SECRET GRANTHAM

John Pinchbeck

AMBERLEY

First published 2018

Amberley Publishing
The Hill, Stroud
Gloucestershire, GL5 4EP

www.amberley-books.com

Copyright © John Pinchbeck, 2018

The right of John Pinchbeck to be identified as the
Author of this work has been asserted in accordance
with the Copyrights, Designs and Patents Act 1988.

ISBN 978 1 4456 7650 0 (print)
ISBN 978 1 4456 7651 7 (ebook)

British Library Cataloguing in Publication Data.
A catalogue record for this book is available from the
British Library.

Origination by Amberley Publishing.
Printed in Great Britain.

Contents

Preface 5

1. Welcome to Grantham 6

2. Law, Order and Infrastructure 13

3. Town Centre 32

4. Other Buildings of Interest 46

5. In the Name of God 65

6. Transport 77

7. Into the Suburbs 84

Acknowledgements 95

About the Author 96

SIGILLUM BURGENCIUM ET COMMUNITATIS VILLE DE GRANTHAM

GRANTHAM.

Preface

Although the title of this book is *Secret Grantham*, it is not just about deliberately hidden places but also about the little-known facts of the town. Had it been written by Michael Caine, it would probably have been called *Not a Lot of People Know That!*

Much of the book looks at buildings and items we see every day, of which we know little. For example, there is the estate agents' office that was once the town house of nobility who received royal visitors; the showroom once variously a skating rink, cinema and theatre; and who are those mysterious images carved into the archway of the Angel and Royal Hotel supposed to be? It also looks at why and how we achieved canals, railways, telephone networks, a legal system and 'how we got to now'.

Once I collected these facts, the biggest problem I had was to condense the written words to one quarter of the size; lots of information collected had to be omitted. So who knows? At some time in the future there could be another addition to the series.

Secret Grantham doesn't just cover local history; it asks questions such as where does our water come from and how many patients does Grantham Hospital deal with? It will also reveal some other staggering statistics.

1. Welcome to Grantham

The oldest part of Grantham is Saltersford, the area around the River Witham near Little Ponton, with evidence of life dating from the age of the dinosaurs. This area was covered by shallow seas, and sediments laid down during the Jurassic period, which formed the limestone that runs in a ridge from north to south through the county.

During the Cretaceous period (136 million to 65 million years ago) the dominant group of reptiles in the sea was the plesiosaur. In 1914 the remains of a plesiosaur were uncovered, making Saltersford one of the most significant places for fossil finds in Lincolnshire.

Before the Roman occupation this area was settled by a tribe known as the Corieltauvi. Finds unearthed here from the middle of the first century to AD 423, spanning most of the Roman occupation, indicate this was a thriving settlement.

The remains of a plesiosaur uncovered at Saltersford in 1914.

Well Worth Its Salt

The reason for the importance of this settlement was salt. Many centuries before freezers, salt was an important commodity used for flavouring and preserving both fish and meat, and in other processes including leather manufacturing.

The shallow seawater of the Wash was ideal to extract salt from and salt-working sites were set up around the sixth century BC. Inland tracks were created including the Salters Way, which ran 40 miles from Donington to the Fosse Way, near Melton Mowbray, crossing the Witham by a ford – hence the name Saltersford.

The settlement disappeared after the Romans, to be replaced by another a mile further north along the Witham Valley, around what is now Dysart Park. The reason for this shift is not entirely clear, although the Anglo-Saxons seem to have preferred settling away from the Romans.

Anglo-Saxon burial mounds at Spittlegate suggest a tribe lived in the Spittlegate Mill area from around AD 400. There is also evidence of a settlement to the west of town towards Harlaxton. An aerial survey in the 1990s of the field adjacent to Echo Spinney showed the signs of a small town, possibly Iron Age, although excavations have yet to be carried out.

Grantham grew rapidly and by the time of the Norman Conquest it was a royal borough. The Great North Road (A1) replaced Ermine Street as the main route north, passing through Grantham, ensuring it remained an important communications and trading centre.

Bridge Led to Town's Importance

The beginning of Grantham's economic development had its origins 14 miles away. Little did residents of 1168 Newark realise their decision to build a bridge over the River Trent would put its southern neighbour on the map. It led to the Great North Road (GNR) moving eastwards, and Grantham began serving travellers.

By the late 1600s, long-distance coach and mail services developed as roads became safer and more people travelled following the end of the Civil War. Numerous inns opened in Grantham, especially on High Street, to accommodate travellers and provide fresh horses. Farriers and ostlers found Grantham suddenly had a large customer base. The George, White Hart, Blue Dog, The Mail Inn and Red Lion were built on High Street in the mid- to late 1700s to serve increasing coach traffic, both mail and stage. In the 1820s, the heyday of stagecoach travel, the Royal Charlotte ran between Edinburgh and London, plus the York, Edinburgh and Aberdeen Royal Mail and the York–Leeds Post Coach. Each stopped at The Angel Hotel.

The fastest coach between Grantham and London took sixteen hours.

DID YOU KNOW THAT...?

Plague Raged through Town

The plague raged in Grantham, especially in 1637 during the months of April and May. Registers record the names of sixty-eight people buried in the churchyard in the last three weeks of May. This was the third visitation of the plague in twenty-one years, having also swept through town in 1616 and in 1627.

King John lodged in the town in 1203 and two years later he granted the manor of Grantham to William de Warenne. De Warenne's coat of arms of blue and gold check later formed the coat of arms of Grantham Borough Corporation and remains the town's arms today. The motto *Sigillum Burgencium et Communitatis Ville de Grantham* roughly means the 'seal of the defenders and community of the town of Grantham'. Earle de Warenne owned land to the west of town called Earle's Fields, later becoming Earlesfield.

How Grantham Became a Town

Grantham 'officially' became a town in 1463 under a royal charter granted by Edward IV. Just as a house has deeds to identify its owner, the charter identifies the town as being owned by its people. Having no defences, Grantham was sacked by Lancastrian troops returning from the Battle of Towton during the Wars of the Roses in 1461. As a reward – or compensation – Edward IV awarded Grantham, then belonging to his mother, Cicely, Duchess of York, the charter.

Before that, Grantham was owned by a number of people. It was the dowry for several queens, then held by various lords of the manor. In 1312, John, 5th Earl of Warenne gave the townsmen a charter. This freed them from having to work for the manor and they could appoint an alderman or chief officer. The people could also set what amounted to the council tax of its day and control the production and sale of many things.

There were special assizes for bread, wine and ale as with our Trading Standards. There followed charters from Richard Ill, in 1484, allowing a weekly market on Wednesdays 'forever' and one from Elizabeth I in 1559.

DID YOU KNOW THAT...?

Gift from the King
King James VI of Scotland presented Grantham Corporation with a silver cup in 1604 when visiting the town while on his way south to be crowned King James I of England.

It Just Kept Growing

Just as Stoke-on-Trent is a combination of five towns, the town of Grantham as we know it today is far bigger than it was before the Borough Extension Act of 1879.

If you follow the River Witham from St Catherine's Road bridge to the White Bridge in Wyndham Park, follow the Mowbeck to Harlaxton Road railway bridge, then back along Wharf Road to your starting point, you have more or less walked along the old boundary.

London Road, University Square, Brewery Hill, Commercial Road, Norton and Grantley streets were all in the parish of Spittlegate, which had its own church, court and police force.

To the south-east of Spittlegate was the sparsely populated Houghton with Walton to the west, while to the east was New Somerby where Dudley Road and Harrowby Road now stand. Behind Market Place was The Grange, and to the west lay the Earle's Fields, yet to be populated. North of Brook Street was the notorious Little Gonerby with Vere Court and New Street contrasting with the pleasant Georgian homes on North Parade.

All of these parishes became part of Grantham overnight. Harrowby Lane, Queensway and Cherry Orchard are in the part of the old Harrowby parish which was also absorbed into Grantham. The rest was called 'Harrowby Without' and amalgamated with Londonthorpe.

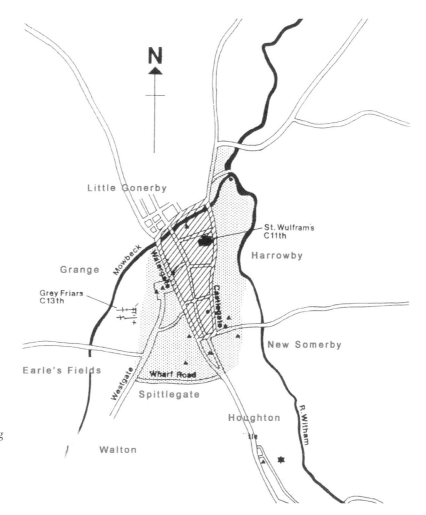

Map showing Grantham in 1878 immediately before surrounding parishes were swallowed up.

The town grew by a further 1,000 hectares in 1930 by absorbing more land from neighbouring parishes, doubling the size of the town. A third of the expansion came from Spittlegate Without, while a quarter was by annexing much of Manthorpe, Gonerby Hill Foot, plus parts of Barrowby and Old Somerby.

The residential Sunningdale area and Alma Park remain outside Grantham, in the parish of Londonthorpe and Harrowby Without.

DID YOU KNOW THAT...?

Grantham: Royal Estate

Records show that in the 1060s the Manor of Grantham formed part of the estates of Queen Edith, wife of King Edward the Confessor, and continued to be in the queen's ownership for several centuries. It remained a royal estate until 1696.

GRANTHAM'S POPULATION

1801	4,288
1821	6,077
1831	7,427
1841	8,691
1851	10,870
1861	11,121
1871	13,225
1881	17,345
1891	16,746
1901	17,593
1911	20,070
1921	18,902
1931	19,630
1951	23,555
1961	25,048
1971	27,943
1981	30,700
1991	33,243
2001	34,592
2011	41,998

It's the Way You Say it

The pronunciation of the town's name has changed, according to Oxford University Press book *The Sounds of Standard English* by J. Nicklin.

It said, 'the termination -ham has suffered developments. Although we may still hear *Grantm* or perhaps better *Grahnt-m*, the pronunciation *Gran-tham* is becoming more and more common.' Now it is more common to hear *Gran-thm* or even *Gran-fm*. The river now pronounced *With-m* was once called *Wit-ham*. And the sound of the district Kesteven is also evolving, from *Kest-ev-en* to *Kest-even* in Lincolnshire [*Lin-cun-shr*].

Two Rivers Run through It

Grantham has two rivers: the Witham and the Mowbeck (or Mow Beck). The smaller of the two, the Mowbeck, rises in the grounds of Harlaxton Manor, runs alongside the canal for a spell, then underground from Old Wharf Road and re-emerges to join the Witham at the White Bridge in Wyndham Park. It once ran openly down the middle of Brook Street.

The main river, the Witham, rises near South Witham, runs north to Lincoln and joins the Wash near Boston. At one time it had two streams running parallel along the Welham Street area. They were made into one in the 1860s after the Queen's (or Welham) Mill was demolished.

The Queen's Mill at the end of Well Lane (now East Street). The ducking stools were for brewers whose beer was not up to standard.

Britain's Most Boring Town

In 1981 Grantham was given the tag it still finds hard to live down even today. Radio 1's *Studio B15*, presented by Adrian Love, staged a vote for the most boring town in Britain. Grantham won hands down with 1,054 votes. Several hundred votes behind was runner-up Hayling Island with Caernarfon in third place.

Receiving the Golden Yawn Award from Mr Love, Mayor of Grantham Paddy Perry said, 'This a fair award for certain sections of the community, but probably not a fair award for the whole community, as I'm happy to accept this award on behalf of those bored people who can't be bothered to get off their backsides and see what's happening.'

2. Law, Order and Infrastructure

Courts and Justice

The system of lay magistrates, by which small crimes are tried, goes back to 1195 – Richard I's reign. He appointed knights known as Keepers of the Peace to ensure the king's peace was upheld.

By Victorian times, most magistrates were members of the borough council, with chairman of the bench often the mayor. It was a throwback to past centuries when the mayor and the first twelve comburgesses ran the town and dispensed justice – a practice which officially disappeared in the 1970s.

Grantham had two magistrates' courts. One was the Grantham division, held at the Guildhall sessions hall, and the other was Spittlegate division, which looked after non-town matters. The latter was administered at the old Court House, London Road, built in 1830 and which at one time doubled as a police station. The superintendent of police also lived there and stabled his horse in outbuildings. Two adjacent cottages in Rycroft Street were home to a sergeant and a constable.

The sessions hall, Guildhall, in the 1920s.

The magistrates' courts in town ran under several names, including Police Court, Borough Court and Petty Sessions. There were also the higher Quarter Sessions, presided over by a visiting recorder in the sessions hall four times a year. More serious offences were dealt with by Lincoln Assizes, replaced by Crown Courts in 1972.

Also that year Spittlegate and Grantham courts merged, taking up residence in the London Road building. A £30,000 improvement in 1978 saw a two-storey extension replace the outmoded offices for the eleven members of staff. Until then, solicitors had to interview clients in the corridor, the clerk shared an office with his deputy and there was no accommodation for probation officers, police or witnesses. There was no holding accommodation for prisoners as the cells were used for storage. The staircase and landing were used as waiting rooms. Staff moved into St Vincent's while improvements were carried out.

Over the years, mergers saw closures of smaller court offices, which led to the creation of South Lincolnshire Magistrates, based in Grantham. An unsuccessful attempt was made to secure the former St John's Vicarage next door. Then in 1995 the former Eddison Plant building, Harlaxton Road, was bought and remained its final home. The last link with the old justice roots in Grantham ended in June 1995 when two fine defaulters were dealt with at the old Spittlegate Court building before the studded door was locked and the building put up for sale at £165,000. It was taken over by Belvoir Properties.

In June 2016, Grantham court and its offices closed and work transferred, mainly to Lincoln.

Police

Grantham's first professional police force began on 9 February 1836 with four constables and a chief constable. They were based at the Guildhall in Guildhall Street, and until 1861 the chief constable was also governor of the prison. It was reorganised by the council in 1857, and was headed by a superintendent with two first-class constables at £1 per week, three second class at 90p and one third class at 80p.

The superintendent, whose salary was £80 per year, also acted as inspector of weights and measures, nuisances, fire engines, inspector of lodging houses, and was responsible for cleaning the sessions hall.

When the town boundaries were extended in 1879 the borough and Spittlegate forces combined, bringing the strength up to three sergeants, ten constables and a chief constable.

In 1929, a new police station was built near the Guildhall and when the bus station was opened some six years later, it was a prominent feature. Grantham Borough Police lost its identity in April 1947 when it amalgamated with the Lincolnshire Constabulary, later known as Lincolnshire Police. Shortage of space forced them to move again in 1959 when they took over Stonebridge, St Catherine's Road, which had recently been vacated by Spittlegate School. They moved to a purpose-built £9.2 million home on Swingbridge Road on 2007.

Police station at the bus station, St Peter's Hill, in the 1950s. (Photo courtesy of David Kettle)

This timber building in a Grantham garden off Dysart Road may look like any other garden shed, but it was once the police holding cells, rescued when the former police station near the Guildhall closed in the 1950s.

Holding cell at Stonebridge police station.

DID YOU KNOW THAT...?

Police Driven Loco

Police whistles were replaced by rattles in the 1850s because it was hard to distinguish between police whistles and the whistles of locomotives on the newly arrived railway. Chief Constable Howard said, 'It's caused a lot of confusion for both us and the railways.'

DID YOU KNOW THAT...?

Police Hot under the Collar

Grantham police were provided with battery lamps for night duties in 1912. The former oil lamps they had been using often caused illness. They also got very hot underneath the officers' capes and gave off fumes.

Grantham's Great Fires

Grantham is well served by a professional firefighting and rescue service – but it wasn't always that way.

The Great Fire of London in 1666 created the first fire brigades. These were run by insurance companies and only put out the fires of their clients. Towns like Grantham still had to rely on neighbours passing buckets of water to each other, drawn from the river or the nearest pump. (At Stamford, smoking in the street was banned to reduce fire risk.)

In 1663, three years before the Great Fire of London, a serious fire destroyed many of Grantham's timber-framed buildings. Forty-three buildings went up in smoke and nearly 400 residents were left homeless. The population at the time was around 2,200. The town centre was rebuilt mainly in stone. A century later the block of buildings between Butchers Row and Guildhall Street was razed to the ground by another blaze. Among the casualties was an inn called le George. In its place the building we knew as the George Hotel (and later as the George Centre) was erected within ten years.

Another fire, in 1706, 'burnt downe and consumed 17 dwelling houses and many barnes, stables and outhouses and goods in warehouses and other places'. Damage was put at many thousands of pounds.

The first local volunteer fire brigade, based in the north porch of St Wulfram's Church, was formed in 1764 as a result of yet another major fire which left up to 400 citizens homeless. Yet it was pretty basic as when the Corn Exchange, High Street, burned down a century later, they still used a bucket chain from the Conduit in Market Place.

The victim still had to pay for the service. Included in the charge was a pint of ale and sandwiches for each fireman.

Then in 1886 the fire station moved to the Guildhall and the borough council established the first official volunteer brigade. The first move towards a modern fire service was in 1891 when firemen had bells fitted in their homes. Gradually, they moved on from horse-drawn steam pumps – horses were finally replaced in 1925 – to the self-contained units we have to today. The final move was to Harlaxton Road in 1946. The building was replaced on the same site in 1972.

Several of the local factories also had their own fire brigades, notably Richard Hornsby's Ironworks. In 1906 at the major fire at Denton Manor, they were first on the scene (mainly because their volunteers were all on the same site). Their fire station still stands on London Road, now occupied by National Tyres.

Putting Out the Moon

A notable episode in the history of the town's fire brigade was in 1892 when they tried to 'put out the moon'. They arrived at the top of Hall's Hill after being summoned by a group of men who had been 'imbibing generously at a local hostelry' and saw what they thought was a hedge fire. The crew trained their hoses on it with no effect. Then one of them looked behind the hedge to discover it was the moon.

This led to the nickname Grantham Toms (the equivalent of right Charlies) and the event was commemorated on postcards as well as the brigade's own Christmas card.

Comic postcard of the Grantham Toms 'putting out the Moon'.

Grantham General Hospital

Grantham Hospital was officially opened by Lady Brownlow in 1876. The Gothic-style, two-storey building had two wings, one for each sex, with seven beds each plus a nurses' room.

The building was paid for by public donations including a £1,000 gift from Earl of Dysart and the land by Earl Brownlow. But ten years after opening it was in urgent need of repairs. Rain began leaking through the roof in all parts of the building. Flaws were discovered in walls and flooring had to be replaced.

A children's ward behind the main hospital was opened in 1889 by Mrs Bradshaw-Isherwood, who also donated more than £300.

The first big expansion came in 1935. The six wards each had a kitchen, a sisters' room and a room for a private nurse was built at the end of the corridor. Being pre-NHS, the charge for each room was set at 75p per day or a subscription of £2.10 per year. Pay beds were also available in the children's ward at £3.15 per week. Medical fees were extra and by arrangement between the patient and doctor.

In 1938, there was a crisis in maternity. Chairman Rothwell Lee said there were only ten beds in the labour ward serving a population of 40,000.

In 1946, another crisis beset the hospital. Secretary John E. Ray said there were thirty-five nursing vacancies for an establishment of sixty staff. He blamed the difficulty on foreign and Commonwealth nurses getting passports and visas to come the Britain.

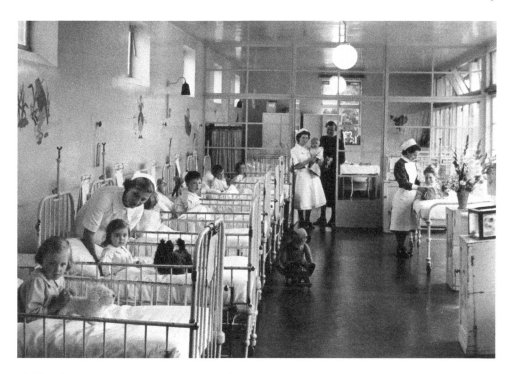

Children's surgical ward, Grantham Hospital, in the 1940s.

Grantham Hospital from the maternity wing, taken in the 1970s.

A £196,000 development of three wards, a new nurses' home, a boiler house and engineer's department were opened at Grantham Hospital in 1961.

In 1972, the new £440,000 three-storey maternity-gynaecology department opened, with four-star hotel amenities. Originally, the department was designed to take forty-eight maternity cases plus ten cots for special care babies, but an unpredicted fall in the birth rate caused hospital bosses to cut this to thirty-six cases, making room for sixteen beds in the gynaecology unit.

Waiting lists reached critical levels in 1977 with more than 1,500 people awaiting inpatient treatment. This included 324 for orthopaedic surgery, 365 for gynaecological surgery and a further 666 for general surgery.

The next crisis came in 1991, when following the Beverly Allitt murders, Nottingham's Queen's Medical Centre took over children's services at Grantham Hospital. Allitt, a nurse at Grantham Hospital, was convicted of murdering four children, attempting to murder three other children, and causing grievous bodily harm to a further six. Then in 1996, when maternity services were threatened and other services downgraded, 1,300 people turned up to object at a meeting in St Wulfram's Church. The following year protesters marched through Grantham registering their anger at plans to close the town hospital's children's ward. Waving placards and chanting 'save our hospital', the demonstrators marched to the hospital where they held a vigil for the afternoon.

The next crisis loomed in 2016, when hospital bosses shut the night services for the Accident and Emergency Department. There were several marches, demonstrations at Westminster, and a weekly night-time vigil by activists.

Vigil outside Grantham Hospital in 2007, protesting at A&E overnight closure.

In 2016/17, Grantham Hospital dealt with 14,465 inpatients, 88,344 outpatients, 24,800 were dealt with in A&E and 1,282 operations were carried out. The highest in any single day during the same period were eighty-two inpatients, 489 outpatients, 126 by A&E and thirty-three operations.

DID YOU KNOW THAT...?

Hospital on the Phone
In 1930, town councillor Ald Rowe said Grantham Hospital should be provided with a telephone as 'It is vital in case of serious illness or fire.'

Other Hospitals
The first hospital in Grantham was on what is now London Road. Workmen digging foundations for factory extensions near Hornsby's Spittlegate Ironworks in 1874 (now the site of the filling station on London Road) discovered forty-two human remains. A bullet found in the skull of one of the skeletons indicated they were soldiers who fought in the Civil War in 1643. It was also the site of St Leonard's Hospital founded by King David of Scotland for pilgrims going to the Holy Land. Industrialist Richard Hornsby, who owned the land, ordered the coffins to be preserved and the bones reburied at the cemetery.

In 1991, contractors excavating for St Leonard's petrol station on the site had to stop work when they unearthed a further fifty skeletons. Archaeologists confirmed these were part of the thirteenth-century leper colony.

A pest house stood to the east of Manthorpe Road, close to what is now Slate Mill Place. It was first referred to in 1584. This was the equivalent of an isolation hospital, where people with infectious diseases were sent, although not treated. The last mention of the building was in the 1851 census.

At one time there was an isolation hospital on Gorse Lane, known locally as the Fever Tents, for patients with infectious and contagious diseases, especially scarlet fever. It opened in 1895 and one of its first casualties was a nurse called Annette, who caught scarlet fever from a patient.

The buildings found a new lease of life in 1951 when it became a Youth Hostel but closed in 1957 when the YHA moved to Dudley Road. It was demolished to make way for Lazy Acres caravan site and is now a private property.

The junction of New Beacon Road and Harrowby Lane is often referred to as Pensions Corner, after the hospital that stood there. It was set up by the Ministry of Pensions in 1921. Predating New Beacon Road, it was set in 15 acres, and utilised much of the former officers' mess at the former Harrowby Army Camp.

Serving the East Midlands, it could house up to 300 patients, each ward having twenty beds. Patients had their own cricket and bowls teams.

The Ministry of Pensions Hospital, Harrowby Lane, in 1923.

It closed in 1930 and patients were transferred to Orpington, while Grantham Hospital was expanded five years later.

Water Water Everywhere

The stone structure in the corner of Market Place was once the main source of fresh water in Grantham. Known as the Conduit, it was the town's first piped water supply.

In medieval Grantham there were at least four public wells. Springwater was also available, brought through lead pipes from a source in a field near today's Winchester Road. The Greyfriars were given permission to lay lead pipes the half-mile from the spring to the priory from 1314. The Conduit was one of the major sources of clean water for the town well into the nineteenth century.

Grantham Waterworks Company was formed in 1849 to establish a new and sufficient supply of pure water for Grantham. The town had more than doubled in size and the only fresh water was from wells.

By 1851 springs at Sproxton, 4 miles south of the town, were connected to a pipeline that fed into a new underground reservoir on Spittlegate Hill, from which mains were laid to the rapidly growing town. However, this new supply soon proved inadequate.

The waterworks company gained the right to use springs in the parishes of Great and Little Ponton, and in 1873 an Act of Parliament granted the water of the Cringle Brook to the people of Grantham. A pipeline carried the water to Saltersford, where a pumping station was built with storage reservoirs and sand filters. From that time the site has continually developed, leading to today's modern, computer-controlled treatment works. A new reservoir was excavated at Saltersford in 1924 and massive rebuilding took place in the early 1980s.

The disused underground reservoir on Spittlegate Hill.

Work on creating the waterworks, Saltersford, in the 1880s.

Grantham Waterworks, Saltersford, today.

The town and surrounding area now draws around 90 per cent of its water from Rutland Water and 10 per cent from Cringle Brook, which enters a reservoir at Saltersford by a cascade to aerate it, then has ozone pumped into it. It then flows through a series of filters and various chemicals are added.

Water from Saltersford is pumped through a series of reservoirs – there are two on Gorse Lane and one at the top of Harrowby Lane, each holding a million gallons, plus water towers – to serve 80,000 people in the Grantham area, which stretches from Claypole in the north to South Witham.

Saltersford treats, on average, around 22 million litres of water a day – enough to fill 275,000 baths. In 1935 the figure was 4.5 million litres.

Gas comes to Grantham

The gasworks was built by the Grantham Gaslight and Coke Co. on the east bank of the Grantham Canal in around 1833. Its site was to facilitate the delivery of coal. Later, a siding was constructed from the Ambergate railway at the canal basin.

It was mainly to supply gas for lighting factories (which were mainly in that part of town) or the more affluent homes. Gas street lamps were introduced in the 1850s. It wasn't until late Victorian times that middle- and working-class homes were converted. Up until then they used either oil lamps or tallow candles – which were rather smelly. Gas wasn't used for heating until the early twentieth century.

Grantham Gasworks in the 1930s.

Grantham gasworks was enlarged in 1900 and many homes were converted to gas lighting. Production ceased in 1953 with the advent of North Sea Gas and the site was demolished in 1958. All that remains is the old access road from Harlaxton Road called Gasworks Lane.

Power to the People

Electricity arrived in Grantham in 1868. It was undertaken by the Urban Electric Supply Co. Yet fourteen years later it hadn't caught on, save for a few businesses such as ironmongers J. Martin and Son, which had its own generators powered by Hornsby engines.

In 1903 Grantham's first power station in East Street was switched on. The generators were able to supply businesses and private houses in High Street, Watergate, London Road, Wharf Road, Westgate, Castlegate and Swinegate. Electricity was available between dusk and 11 p.m. although it was planned to be continuous. The power came from two Grantham-built 90hp Hornsby water tube boilers.

Two cables ran up East Street to Castlegate, one going north and the other south. It was not long before the council preferred all new lighting to be electric and gas street lighting was gradually replaced. This accelerated in the late 1940s and new electric standards were erected by prisoners of war.

By 1950 work began on a £14,000 scheme to replace all of Grantham's gas street lamps with electric ones, even the traditional 'dolphin' gas lamp standards.

As more and more consumers joined up, the Grantham power station could no longer cope and Grantham was supplied off the National Grid.

The generator room at Grantham Power Station, East Street, in the early 1900s.

Telephone Exchange, Market Place

The telephone, invented in 1876, began to take off in England in 1881. The first in Grantham was for businessman William Carlon in 1885. Even in 1901 there were only thirty-three subscribers in town, but the council agreed to spend £2,000 on a telephone exchange in Market Place which would link up with the National Telephone Company, in the belief this could reach eighty people. Cables were overhead and it wasn't until 1923 that the council gave operator the General Post Office permission to lay town centre cables underground.

As needs grew Post Office Telephones, as it was called in 1934, erected phone kiosks on South Parade and at the corner of Station Road and Harlaxton Road.

Connections were by operators who worked above the General Post Office, St Peter's Hill. In 1953, twenty-four girls worked between 8 a.m. and 6 p.m., with seventeen men taking over the night shift. Together they handled 5,000 calls a day, out of which 2,000 of them were local calls. At peak times they handled 500 calls an hour. This was at bursting point in 1964 as subscribers had reached 2,250, so a new exchange was built in Inner Street for the introduction of STD (subscriber trunk dialling).

But as more and more automation was introduced, manual work declined and in 1992 the telephone exchange closed and work transferred to Peterborough. The building is now used by telephone engineers.

Telephone exchange at General Post Office, St Peter's Hill, in 1953.

Postal Services

The first post office in Grantham was at the Angel Hotel from around 1690, although it appeared to have moved elsewhere on High Street by 1826. It relocated to Market Place, although this was not necessarily a good move. In 1893, a sanitary inspector who visited the premises told the authorities to look for somewhere new as it was in 'an unsanitary, rat-infested condition'.

Today's post office (far right) shortly after it opened in 1969 and its predecessor about to be demolished, taken in 1960.

It moved across the road for a spell, then took over Boots pharmacy, London Road, until specially built premises on Peter's Hill, the site where one still stands, was completed in 1922.

The main post office we know today was built in 1969 and followed the standard house design.

DID YOU KNOW THAT...?

Grantham Gets Streetwise

Nameplates were installed on all streets and all houses were numbered in 1871, helping postmen with deliveries. The work was carried out at the request of the census office. Because of the rapid development in the town, many streets had to be renumbered in 1914.

Workhouses

Union Street derived its name from Grantham's first workhouse in Trigg's Yard, which runs between Watergate and Union Street. It was built on the site of the Red Lion inn, which had been given to the town by Francis Trigg (or Trigge) in 1597 to support the poor.

For centuries, Grantham's poor were well looked after through various bequests from well-to-do residents. A report in 1777 shows there were sixty inmates at the Union Workhouse, in Trigg's Yard. Then the Poor Law Amendment Act of 1834 set up the union workhouse system. For orphaned children, widows, the elderly and the mentally ill who could not support themselves, or had no family, the dreaded workhouse was where they ended up.

Then in 1838, a 300-bed workhouse was built in Spittlegate at a cost of £6,000, roughly around where the Railway Club now stands. The hexagonal-shaped workhouse, with a central supervision hub, was run by a Board of Guardians. Food was basic: porridge, coarse dark bread, gruel, cheese and occasionally a little meat, although even this was often better than meals of the poorest labourers' families. Life inside was grim, with those capable expected to undertake laborious work.

When the new workhouse on Dysart Road opened in 1892, costing £13,500, the old one became a temporary mental hospital while the asylum was being built at Rauceby. During the First World War it was a military hospital, then sold to the Great Northern Railway for £13,500 and demolished.

The new one, known as Hill View, stood in 10 acres of ground that stretched to the Grantham Canal.

It was taken over by Kesteven County Council in 1929, signalling the end of the workhouse system. The building was developed as Hill View hospital for the chronically sick, and as a maternity hospital. In 1964, forty-four chronically sick patients were moved from Hill View, and once the new maternity wing at Grantham Hospital was complete, the complex closed. The buildings were demolished in the 1970s to make way for Harrison House old people's home.

DID YOU KNOW THAT...?

Unhealthy Women at Workhouse

A report into Grantham Workhouse in 1862 said, 'There are three low one-storey buildings used for the itch, syphilis, and offensive cases among women; but some are retained in the ordinary wards.'

The former Hill View workhouse in 1953.

Public Library

Grantham Library moved to its present site in the newly built Isaac Newton Centre in 1984. The £238,000 library was then the biggest in Lincolnshire and at 12,000 sq ft, was three times the size of the former building. There were 30,000 books on the shelves, and room for half as many again.

Grantham's first purpose-built public library and museum opened in May 1926, on the ground floor of what became the museum. In the first two days, 861 books were lent.

The first library in town, excluding the Trigg's chained library in the parish church, was at the Philosophical Institution, Finkin Street, between 1840 and1858. There was also a library in the Exchange Hall, Westgate, and later in the Guildhall, but these were not for general public use.

A free public library had first been mooted in 1893 but a vote among townsfolk saw 460 in favour and 1,729 against, although a further vote in 1911 was won 1,562 votes to 960. The war intervened before anything was done, but in 1922 it was finally established

DID YOU KNOW THAT...?

Disquiet over Western Front

There was outcry among readers at Grantham Public Library in 1930 when town councillors banned a top-selling book from the library. Three separate petitions were raised protesting at the refusal to stock E. M. Remarque's *All Quiet on the Western Front*. Councillors said it was 'unsuitable' for the town's readers as it observed the First World War from the German side.

The children's library in 1934.

in temporary quarters on St Peter's Hill, partly funded by the Carnegie UK Trust grant of £4,900. By 1931 there were 2,801 adult members borrowing 72,813 books.

By 2008/09 160,649 books were borrowed, although this was down on the 197,167 of two years earlier. Other media are also more popular now, with 7,900 DVDs and 2,160 CDs lent out as well as 6,100 talking books.

In 2016/17, books were down to 126,870, there were 3,177 DVDs loaned out and three CDs (no longer stocked). Talking books amounted to 3,601.

Cemetery

A shortage of land led to the opening of Grantham Cemetery on Harrowby Road in 1857. The site, St Catherine's Fields, was needed as other town graveyards, especially Manthorpe Road, reached bursting point.

The first burial service at the new cemetery was conducted by the Revd F. Jesson of Spittlegate parish. The following day the Revd Tempest interred the first Roman Catholic.

Mr Haynes, the gravedigger, said that after digging down 1.5 metres on the first grave he first hit a spring, which began to flood his excavation, then struck rock, which he believed to be a metre thick. By 1862 an order was made by the Burial Board for all graves at Grantham Cemetery to be dug more than 2 metres deep to allow two burials from the same family.

Changing fashions by 1966 led to the opening of the £52,000 crematorium. In 1992 it was given a £200,000 facelift, bringing it into line with the latest laws. The two new cremators brought the unit into line with gas emission regulations.

3. Town Centre

Once a Wilderness

Now regarded as the centre of town, in 1850 St Peter's Hill was in such poor condition that it was known as 'The Wilderness', although the official name was Wood Hill. It was the site of a wood mill and timber yard in the eighteenth century – hence its name, although years earlier it had been home to St Peter's Chancel. Once it was tidied up for the statue of Sir Isaac Newton, followed by building the Guildhall, it became more like the area we know today.

Thirteenth-century Landmark Wrecked by Rebels

An Eleanor Cross was erected at the northern end of St Peter's Hill in memory of Queen Eleanor who died at Harby, near Lincoln, in 1290.

The Widow of King Edward I, her funeral cortege rested overnight at Grantham as it made its twelve-day journey to Westminster Abbey for a state funeral service. A cross was built at each resting place.

Grantham's Eleanor Cross was erected in 1300 but was destroyed in 1645 by Parliamentary soldiers in the Civil War, when the town was garrisoned under Colonel Rossiter. It is now commemorated by a plaque on the side of the Guildhall. The Alderman's Court, held in February 1646, ordered the town constables to recover as many stones as possible from the cross on St Peter's Hill from people who had taken them for their own use, and to lay them in the church.

The plaque commemorating Eleanor of Castile on the side of the Guildhall, installed by Grantham Civic Society in 2015.

Who's the Other Bloke?

Everyone knows the Sir Isaac Newton statue, but many people still ask 'who's the other chap?'

The Hon. Frederick James Tollemache, whose statue stands at the southern end of the green, was very popular in his day. He was Member of Parliament for Grantham for forty years, this role spread over four periods between 1826 and 1874. The bronze statue, on a base of granite blocks, cost around £1,700, which was raised by public subscription. Many poor people gave pennies they could ill afford. Tollemache was born at Buckminster Park in 1804, the fifth son and the tenth child of William, Lord Huntingtower. Educated at Harrow, he was elected as a Liberal at the age of twenty-two, one of the two MPs for Grantham.

A lead case is buried beneath the statue. It contains copies of the *Grantham Journal*, *Grantham Times*, *Lincolnshire Herald*, *London Times*, names of councillors and town officials, coins of 1891 including a silver five-shilling piece (25p), a short biography of Tollemache and a list of ninety-six people who contributed more than £1, and 200 who gave from three pence to 10 shillings to the statue fund.

In 1897, when no one wanted to be the mayor of Grantham, jokers made their own mayoral chain and hung it around the statue's neck.

Market Millennium

Grantham has had a market for more than 1,000 years and for a long time had two. In Saxon times and for almost 300 years after the Norman Conquest it was west of St Wulfram's Church, just off Swinegate. It was moved in around 1280 after Pope Innocent III decreed that markets should not be too close to churches.

The right to hold the Saturday market was in the hands of the lords of the manor until 1484 when in his charter Richard III gave permission to 'to hold a market in the town every week for ever on every Wednesday'.

In 1634, Queen Henrietta Maria, wife of Charles I, leased the market rights to the town council. The Wednesday market ended to avoid competition with the one at Newark. This left the Saturday market profits in the hands of the lords of the manor.

In the 1800s there was a cattle market, fish market and cloth market. On St Peter's Hill there was a horse market until the turn of the twentieth century. A pig market was held on Saturday mornings in Wide Westgate outside the Blue Bull pub until shortly after the Second World War. In 1870 the town council tried to buy the rights of the market from Buckminster Estate. They were turned down.

The cross in Market Place is not religious but merely marked the place where market tolls were payable. It was pulled down by John Manners, Lord of the Manor, in 1779, but an action was brought by Alderman Thomas Stanser against him for the trespass, and Manners was compelled to restore it in the following year as royal proclamations were to be made from it.

That didn't stop his son William repeating the feat in 1796, but again he was forced to put it back. The Manners family tried yet again in 1884 when this time they replaced it with a granite obelisk.

In 1910 the cross was returned and re-erected following a campaign by deputy mayor William Plumb. When the obelisk was taken down, a large screw-top bottle was found

Grantham Market Place in 1805 with the original cross.

The obelisk that replaced the market cross for some years.

containing what at first appeared to be dust. Closer inspection revealed a copy of the *Grantham Journal,* which gave an account of the proposed monument. In the centre of the cross today is a copper case containing three copper plates and a sealed jar containing a copy of the *Grantham Journal.*

The Oxford Street shrine installed in 1917. Little trace remains of this today.

Shrine to Remember the Street's War Dead

Oxford Street residents erected a shrine in 1917 in honour of the men from the street serving in the armed forces. The marble tablet bore the names of those both serving and killed. It was organised by Mrs Shaw and Mrs Brown and was unveiled by the Mayor of Grantham, Sir Arthur Priestley MP. At the end of the ceremony, the large crowd gave three rousing cheers, first for the two housewives, then for those the shrine was honouring.

What happened to the shrine remains a mystery.

A Cosy Reminder of PM's Father

Behind the hoarding above the Cosy Corner Café on the corner of London Road and Cambridge Street you can just make out Clifford's Provisions. Grocer Charles Clifford also had a shop in Market Place.

A young Alfred Roberts, the father-to-be of Baroness Thatcher, came from Northamptonshire as an assistant here, before managing the Market Place store. He left in 1919 after buying the now iconic corner shop on North Parade. The first floor of Clifford's London Road shop was a sergeant's mess for the 6th Airborne Division during the Second World War.

The Cosy Corner Café, with a hoarding almost hiding Clifford's store sign.

Watergate: Home to Shoemakers

Watergate, as it was originally and now known, is the way to the water, as the open Mowbeck ran at the bottom of the hill. It was changed in medieval times to Walkergate, although in the early nineteenth century the name reverted.

It was on the old Great North Road before the Grantham bypass opened in 1963 and until the 1950s was very narrow.

Declaring Watergate unfit for modern traffic in 1931, the borough council revealed plans for a widening scheme. A 40-foot line was drawn on the west side of the map, preventing any future development inside it, to allow for road improvements.

Many old houses and shops on the east side were demolished in the 1950s to widen the road. Three buildings at the top of the road, D. H. Sharpley, J. S. Stanton and the Strathdon Hotel, were also pulled down.

At first the area was grassed, apart from the new building known as Watergate House. It then became a car park.

In 1967 it was the turn of the west side when several buildings were demolished to make way for Key Markets superstore.

Watergate east side in 1960, before the bulldozers moved in to widen the road and create a car park.

West side of Watergate, demolished in 1967 to make way for Key Markers (later Lidl). (Photo courtesy of Eric Summers)

Whipples Garage, High Street, in 1912.

Motor Dealer Pharmacy

Whipple's opened its Watergate haberdashery business in around 1882 and was one of the largest in town. Then in 1906, George Whipple opened a garage opposite the George Hotel, to cater for the new, expanding interest in motor cars.

In June 1916, the Watergate drapers was destroyed in a mystery £15,000 blaze. Only the outer walls remained of the three storey-building. Looking to the future, Whipple rebuilt a garage on the haberdashery site in 1920. It was set back from the road to allow forecourt parking. At nearly 200m long, it was the biggest garage workshop in the eastern counties, able to store 300 cars. Eventually, and for many years, it was Grantham's Vauxhall dealership.

It closed in 1986 and was taken over by exhaust and tyre specialists Kwik Fit.

The original garage became Geo Mills outfitters, and is now a pharmacy.

Skating Rink to Showroom

Erected as a showroom for Boyall's carriages in the 1860s, this Wharf Road building has come full circle and is now a builders' merchants.

Following the closure of Boyall's, it was used by the Lincolnshire Regiment as an orderly room for a time in the 1880s and then became the Premier (roller-skating) Rink.

After major alterations it reopened in 1911 as the King's Picture Palace with 800 seats. The floor was inclined steeply from the rear to give an unrestricted view of the screen from all parts of the cinema and the former bandstand was converted into a private box.

Former roller-skating rink on Wharf Road.

Projection equipment was run by electricity. The first film to be shown was *Beautiful Galliano*. Other films on the opening programme included *Our Topical Gazette, Glimpses of Old China, Man and his Ma-in-Law* and *Our Tilly Goes to Skegness*.

It closed in 1918 due to competition from the Electric Palace, Picture House, Empire and Garrison Theatres.

It was taken over by the YMCA and local dramatic societies before returning to commercial use as timber merchants Coultas and more recently Jewsons.

Angel and Royal Hotel

The Angel, as it was originally called, is one of the oldest buildings in Grantham as well as one of the oldest hostelries in the UK. Once a meeting place for the Knights Templar, the name itself offered protection to travellers. The Templars were also the owners until it was seized by the Sheriff of Lincolnshire in 1308, in accordance with a writ issued by Edward II.

After it was rebuilt, both in the fourteenth and fifteenth century, Richard III visited and signed the death warrant of his cousin the Duke of Buckingham in 1483. At the time, the large room over the gateway was called La Chambre le Roi (the King's Chamber) and probably named after King John's visit in 1213, where he held court. It is now a restaurant. The ill-fated Charles I also stayed there in 1633.

It was a visit in 1866 by the Prince of Wales, later Edward VII, which saw the name changed to the Angel and Royal (Bertie's Bistro is also named after the prince). It was a notable coaching inn in the early nineteenth century, before the railways.

On either side of the entry arch off High Street are carved heads of Edward III and Queen Philippa of Hainault, whose intervention saved the burghers of Calais from certain death. They have eroded to an unrecognisable state.

Above: Angel and Royal in 1833.

Left: The secret staircase discovered at the Angel and Royal by builders in the 1960s.

In 1947, workmen discovered a 9-foot wide fourteenth-century fireplace in a front bar. Then builders working on the King's Room (La Chambre le Roi) in 1964 discovered a hitherto unknown stone spiral staircase.

After being in private hands for many years, the hotel was taken over by a succession of hotel chains, which saw a deterioration and by the 1990s English Heritage was so concerned they put it on their at risk register. Then a group of local businessmen, led by accountant John Hindmarch, bought the hotel for £670,000 from Greene King and set about restoration. It is now owned by a private hotelier.

DID YOU KNOW THAT...?

The golden angel holding a crown over the archway entrance to the Angel and Royal Hotel depicts Archangel St Michael. It is attributed to the patronage of Edward IV, following the visit to the inn by his brother Richard III, who held court there.

Grantham Had Two Corn Exchanges

Westgate Hall, built as a Corn Market in 1852, was given a fresh lease of life as a butter and poultry market in November 1892.

Unusually Grantham had two corn exchanges and both were built and opened the same year as the Great Northern Railway came to Grantham.

Westgate Hall has been used for many things and events, especially during the Second World War. Dances, boxing bouts, sales, meals, political meetings, auctions and a NAAFI club during the last war have all taken place there. In 1948 it was a popular dance hall – but strictly teetotal. It was auction rooms in the 1980s and then became a nightclub in 1993. The club's numerous name changes included Jaspers and Club IT.

The High Street Corn Exchange also became the Central Cinema in 1912 but had been an occasional cinema long before as well as providing live entertainment. Shortly after it opened it had a diorama (the forerunner of the hologram) worth £2,000 (£200,000 in today's money). Crowds flocked to see moving pictures there in 1905 provided by the Japanese Waragraph Animated Picture Co.

The main hall, used by corn merchants, was brightly decorated in 1909. Statues were painted ivory while the glass roof was painted white so corn merchants could show their samples to their best advantage.

Although called the Central Cinema, it was locally known as either the Eccy (Corn Exchange) or the Flea Pit, but it still functioned as an exchange and the cinema seats had to be stacked away during that use. It closed in 1951 after showing *Slattery's Hurricane*.

Without the dual use, the Corn Exchange also closed and the building was converted into a shop, eventually becoming British Heart Foundation's furniture shop.

The Central Cinema from the High Street entrance in 1953 (left) and the entrance to the Corn Exchange, Elmer Street North.

Tudor Café

The Tudor café, formerly known as Catlins, dates from 1560. A pleasant olde worlde restaurant, it is regarded as the spiritual home of the Grantham Gingerbread. During the old coaching days, while the horses were being changed nearby, passengers would stroll down the street and invariably purchase a supply of whetstones – the type of biscuits offered for sale.

Catlins a century ago.

A second-floor room inside Catlins – renamed the Tudor – today.

Then, in 1740, Butchers Row's William Egglestone went into his shop one Sunday morning to procure the ingredients for making small cakes for his family. In the gloom of his shuttered shop he mistook one ingredient for another, and it was not until the cakes were baking he discovered his mistake. The cakes, before being placed in the oven, were cut out with a wine glass, and should have remained that size when baked. Instead, they rose up and became nearly twice the size.

His family liked their delicate flavour, so he made more, this time offering them for sale in his shop calling them Grantham Gingerbread. Being still in the days of the old stagecoaches, travellers bought them readily and so they soon replaced the tasteless Whetstones as their fame spread north and south on the Great North Road.

They spelled prosperity for Mr Egglestone, who on retirement sold his recipe to a tradesman called Merchant Briggs who passed on the recipe to his two daughters. They in turn passed it to their nephew R. S. Bestwick, and his successors, Catlin Bros, who opened a cafe in 1904. It is now Tudors Restaurant & Wine Bar.

George Hotel

Now a shopping centre, the George was once the town's leading hotel. It began as Le George (or Saint George), which Richard, Duke of York bought and leased in 1456. When the duke died in 1460, his son, King Edward IV, gave the George, together with the lordship of Grantham, to his mother, Cicely, Duchess of York.

The original hostelry was destroyed in a major blaze from Butchers Row to Guildhall Street in the 1770s, after which the huge Georgian edifice we know today was built on the site. The sheer size of this imposing building suggests the grand plan was for it to be one side of a Georgian square, with upmarket town houses on the other sides. It had an imposing archway in the centre of the façade which led to a spacious yard and stables.

In the 1820s during the ownership of Sir William Manners it was called George & Blue Boar, a change that does not seem to have lasted many years. During the great era of stagecoach traffic, the inn flourished, and its many visitors included Charles Dickens, who travelled by coach to Greta Bridge in 1838 and wrote to his wife, 'We reached Grantham between 9 and 1 on Tuesday night, and found everything prepared for our reception in the very best inn I have ever put up at.'

In 1923 a ballroom was added and the archway was fitted with a revolving door. It became a quality hotel with forty-six bedrooms, a restaurant and a ballroom for many local functions including wedding receptions, Christmas parties and annual balls. It closed in 1989.

A shopping mall was built on the car park in the 1990s, while the building was converted to shops and offices with a new façade on Guildhall Street. It was named St Peter's Place, but soon reverted to the George Centre.

DID YOU KNOW THAT…?

Increased Traffic
A traffic survey by the Automobile Association in 1924 revealed 1,937 light cars used the A1 in North Street during a week in October. There were also 497 lorries, 544 horse-drawn vehicles and three flocks of sheep or geese. By 2012, this had increased even though the town had been by-passed. A county council survey showed that 13,860 vehicles each day (97,000 a week) travelled the A1, 420 of which were commercials vehicles.

DID YOU KNOW THAT…?

Traffic under Control
Traffic lights were first introduced in Grantham at the Market Place/High Street junction in 1932. At the end of the first week seven motorists appeared before magistrates for ignoring them, including three women drivers who were fined between 5s (25p) and 10s (50p). The next set were installed on St Peter's Hill in 1954, at the five-way junction outside the post office.

Mysterious Crypt

A crypt was discovered under a building in Butchers Row on April 26 1888. This fine example of medieval craftsmanship was 'preserved' by pouring tonnes of concrete on top of it.

At first, it was thought to be part of a former medieval chapel, which by 1789 had become a shoemaker's shop and home. Latterly, however, historians believe is was purely for commercial use, possibly the equivalent of a Middle Ages upmarket wine bar.

Crypt discovered under a building in Butchers Row in April 1888.

DID YOU KNOW THAT....?

Pay to Park Introduced

Motorists had to dip into their pockets to park their cars in Guildhall Street (Greenwoods Row) car park for the first time in 1969. Council workmen put bollards around the car park, leaving only one entrance with a pay kiosk. It also had a height restriction board. Motorists had to pay 1/- (5p) for up to two hours and 2/- (10p) for longer.

4. Other Buildings of Interest

Granta Hall

Usually in the shade of the narrow Finkin Street, you could pass the Grade II building occupied by estate and land agents Brown and Co. without a second glance. It was built in 1836 by the Grantham Philosophical Institution, an organisation dedicated to encourage interest in science and literature, for a mere £1,500. At the rear is a 10-meter-diameter octagonal room, once a library containing 1,200 books. A floor has since been installed in the upper part, now used as a boardroom.

One of two ground-floor committee rooms was occupied by the local Clerical Society and contained a well-stocked theological library. The Philosophical Institution was forced to sell the building in 1859 to pay off its debts.

For many years the building was in mixed use, including as a dispensary where cures were handed out to those paying the penny a week subscription. From 1925 it was occupied by solicitors R. A. White & Son while part of it was the Conservative Club in the 1930s. During the Second World War and for a few years after it was home to the Sky Blue and Khaki Club.

The boardroom of Brown & Co. at Granta Hall.

The circular staircase inside Granta Hall.

Since then it has had a variety of uses, including a printing works. It was during that time, in 1970, that the former schoolroom (Brownlow School and later Girls Central) next door was incorporated into the complex.

Vine Street Cottage

This Grade II-listed stone cottage in Vine Street, which no longer bears a name, is one of the oldest inhabited properties in the town, being built in 1570. Originally a pair of cottages, they were converted into a newsagents and sweet shop called Ye Olde Tuck Shop in 1934. The venture was short-lived and the shop closed in 1942, to become a private house again. It has since returned to commercial use, in antiques.

The former sweet shop at No. 11 Vine Street, owned by John Henry Saville, in 1935.

Spittlegate House, London Road, in the early 1890s.

Spittlegate House

Spittlegate House once stood alone in its extensive grounds.

Built in 1760 by the Revd Thomas Manners of Silk Willoughby, it was owned in the first part of the twentieth century by Dr Charles Frier, who held his surgery there, and after a spell by the Ministry of Pensions it became Strutt & Parker's estate agency.

In 2004, the historic house was converted into affordable housing for young people through Nottingham Community Housing Association. Together with the site of a row of single-storey lock-up shops they produced twenty-three flats.

Grantham House

Inside those forbidding stone walls running along Castlegate is a glorious house and 27 acres of garden, including a meadow and a fine walled garden. There are also two-storey outbuildings, originally stabling, now used as offices and accommodation.

The earliest part of Grantham House, the central hall, was built in around 1370. Both Princess Margaret, sister of Henry VIII and Cardinal Wolsey, lodged there but little remains of the medieval building except some fifteenth-century windows now found on an internal staircase. Most of the building seen today dates from the eighteenth century. The sixteenth-century mullioned windows that look out over the church and entrance front to the north were inserted by the Hall family. (For many years it was called Hall Place after the owners. Hall's Hill is also named after them.)

Above left: The thirteenth-century archway from Grantham House garden, on Castlegate, opposite the steps to St Wulfram's churchyard. It is believed to have come from a building predating Grantham House.

Above right: A lead cistern installed at Grantham House as a gift by the architect during a major refurbishment programme in 1737.

It changed hands several times, and Sir Isaac Newton was about to buy it but died during the transaction.

It was bought by Sir Richard Cust, 2nd Bt of Pinchbeck, in the year of his death, becoming the dower house of his widow, Anne (née Brownlow). In the mid-1730s she transformed the building, adding wings and extra storeys using materials from Belton, turning it into the building we know today. The original is now on the inside of this building.

The house fell into disuse in the early nineteenth century, and was even a school until it was leased to Mr Hutchinson, the Cust's agent. He in turn sublet it to his sister and her husband, the Sedgwick family, in 1884. Mr Sedgwick died within five years, leaving it to his widow and daughters Winifred and Marion.

The Sedgwicks bought the house from the Custs in 1924. The Misses Sedgwick eventually signed it over to the National Trust, including 20 acres of Parkers Field now renamed Sedgwick Meadows.

It was subsequently tenanted by Margaret Thatcher's election agent Major-General Sir Brian Wyldbore-Smith, whose descendants now live there.

DID YOU KNOW THAT...?

Skeleton Discovered

In the early 1970s, tenant Molly Wyldebore Smith was aware of a strange atmosphere in her bedroom at Grantham House. Being psychic, she investigated and after panelling was removed, the skeleton of a young pregnant woman was discovered. It was given a full funeral and the room was exorcised by a priest.

DID YOU KNOW THAT...?

Honoured Guests

Henry VIII's sister Princess Margaret lodged at Hall Place (Grantham House) in 1503 on her way up the Great North Road to Scotland, following her marriage by proxy to James IV, as did Cardinal Wolsey on his last journey north.

DID YOU KNOW THAT...?

Headmistress Fell to Her Death

Grantham House became a finishing school for young ladies in the 1780s. Unfortunately, after ten years, the headmistress either leapt off the roof or fell from an attic window. Either way, that was the end of the school. She is still supposed to haunt the garden. Known as the Grey Lady, the faceless spectre walks at around 6 p.m.

Mystery Mural in House in Church Street

The pre-Georgian building with the uninspired name No. 1 Church Street, on the corner of Castlegate, was acquired by the King's School and turned into its sixth form and business centre. It was formally opened by the Prince of Wales in 1987. The building is believed to be sixteenth century.

An upstairs fire stack has an intriguing mural that was uncovered in 1937, although Freemasons insist it has no relevance to them.

The mural in the Church Street house.

Middlemore House

Today, Middlemore Yard is little more than an area housing the Conservative Club, a car park and a couple of modern homes along the southern side. Almost unnoticed is the stone building that gives it its name.

Middlemore House was built by lawyer Richard Middlemore, born 1658, the son of a Russian merchant. This once stood in spacious grounds and at the end of the eighteenth century had 'a fine and fanciful summer house on the banks of the river, also a Chinese bridge leading to the wilderness, east of the Witham'.

As Grantham developed, Somerby Hall became the family's out-of-town home and the extensive gardens were sold off to build some pretty crude terraced houses.

In 1863, a sanitary inspector, probing various fevers in the yard, said of them, 'We discovered heaps of mud lying around in the main yard with puddles of water. Some privies had sleeping rooms overhead while several families shared the lavatories which were in various states of cleanliness with some as filthy outside as inside. Water and filth had accumulated in the drains and in heaps in the yards and roads.'

In 1912, nine houses in Middlemore Yard, Castlegate, were in such poor condition that the town council ordered the residents out. An order was made prohibiting them to be lived in until they were refurbished and fit to live in. They were all demolished in the 1940s.

Middlemore House has served as a Mr Hardwick's private school, a French polisher's workshop and an Oddfellows lodge meeting place. More recently it has been converted to flats.

Middlemore House, Castlegate.

The slums of Middlemore Yard in the 1930s, now the Conservative Club car park.

Whichcote House, Watergate.

Whichcote House

Whichcote House, Watergate, was originally a private house built in the late 1700s for the dowager Lady Whichcote, whose family lived in the Sleaford area.

Royalty was entertained there. When the Prince of Wales (later George IV) was a guest of Sir Carnaby and Lady Haggerston, of Cheyney House, Castlegate, he and Mrs Maria Fitzherbert would stroll·along the High Street, enjoy a bath bun at Briggs' shop (later Catlins) and call upon Lady Whichcote.

But as Watergate became more commercial, it was converted for retail businesses. Among past tenants were tailor John Burgin, haberdashers Chambers & Co., Halford Cycle Co., Radley Footwear and more recently various estate agents.

St Wulfram's Rectory

St Wulfram's Rectory is one of the most attractive houses in Grantham. Almost perfectly symmetrical, with its Venetian windows, it is a perfect example of Georgian elegance, ideal as a background for a Jane Austen adaptation or, with the addition of snow, a Christmas card.

Yet for the early half of the twentieth century, Regency features were overshadowed by oppressive Victorian wings. Then, the front of the house was obscured by the high wall, where a gate has since been installed. It wasn't until the wings were demolished in 1958 that the Georgian gem was once again exposed in all its glory.

It is on the site – most likely on the cellar – of Dinsdale House, bought by Bishop Sanderson of Lincoln for £100 to house the two Grantham vicars, North and South. The livings were unified in 1714 and in 1789 the old place was pulled down and the present one, designed by John Langwith (who also built Vine House), erected at the cost of £812.

The Rectory, Church Street, with the Revd Christopher Andrews.

Shirley Croft

Shirley Croft was built on Harrowby Road in 1883 for the Lee family of maltsters Lee and Grinling, by Samuel Bentley-Rudd. Henry Bell also owned it in the early twentieth century, but for most of its life has been a hotel.

Shirley Croft shortly before its demolition.

It is named after the field on which it was built. In 1891 lightning struck the south-west of the roof. About 5 metres of rafters were damaged, and although they caught fire they were put out by the rain.

It was bought by a developer in 2007 and demolished for new buildings.

St Vincent's

St Vincent's was built in the Gothic Revival style by industrialist Richard Hornsby in 1865, although he died before he had the chance to move in. Instead, his son Richard Jnr, lived there and it remained in the Hornsby family until 1905.

The trustees sold the house, off Harrowby Road, to Henry Alfred Manners and Henry Bell, who in turn leased it to Percy Farquhar Chandos de Paravacini, who bought it in 1911.

The house was next sold to the Air Council in 1925, for RAF Spitalgate to convert into a regimental institution and barracks, and remained in their possession until after the Second World War. It sprang to fame during the war when it was the headquarters of No. 5 Group RAF Bomber Command and was the nerve centre for the famous Dambusters raids in May 1943, being RAF Bomber Command's No. 5 Group HQ.

In 1943 the United States 9th Air Force took over until December 1945.

The house was sold by auction for £51,000 to Aveling Barford for AB (International) in 1977, then eighteen months later was bought by South Kesteven District Council,

Inside St Vincent's showing the rare marble columns.

Dambusters
Memorial in
the grounds of
St Vincent's.

whose planning department's offices in Sandon Close had been condemned as unsafe. They paid £205,000 plus £1,900 stamp duty. A further £8,000 was spent on furniture and furnishings, £2,500 on structural changes and £8,000 for the car park.

During that time, an outbuilding was employed as a Dambusters museum.

After a short spell as offices for the Magistrates' Court, it was bought by Suter plc in 1987 until Suter was bought out by Ascot nine years later. It has since reverted to a private house.

The Barracks

The Barracks on the corner of Sandon Road, which was then outside of town, was built in 1858, costing £3,640. It comprised a band room over the gateway, a guardroom, a prisoners' room with three cells, two storerooms and even a tailor's shop. There was an armoury for 1,000 rifles and a magazine that could hold 75,000 rounds of ammunition. Either side of the parade ground, which measured 60m by 40m, there were officers' quarters and stables. At the eastern end was a huge covered drill hall.

It was built for the Royal South Lincolnshire Militia, a Victorian forerunner of the Home Guard. The Barracks was extended in 1872 when homes were built for thirty soldiers' families and an adjutant. This became known as Barracks Square and now provides homes for civilians.

The Hollies perform in a very crowded drill hall in the Barracks, Sandon Road, in 1966.

Further along Sandon Road, which until after the First World War was only a footpath, there was an 800-metre rifle range. Later, there was an indoor rifle range behind the drill hall, which was used by the King's School Combined Cadet Force until the 1950s.

During the First World War, the barracks became a Red Cross hospital and was a base for the Home Guard in the Second World War.

After various non-military uses, the 1950s saw it become a social venue with dances held at the drill hall. Artistes ranged from John Dankworth Orchestra to The Who, Cream, The Hollies, the Walker Brothers and English Dogs.

It was taken over by the county education service for KGGS and Grantham College. Then in 1988, the college was told to leave so the county council could sell it for an estimated £250,000.

Now known as The Old Barracks, it is now owned by property company Autumn Park and houses a number of small businesses.

In 1998 it became a Grade II-listed building, as an 'interesting example of domestic planning to provide secure accommodation'.

The White House

Inside the house White House, which dominates Brownlow Street, there is a surprise around every corner, from Queen Ann panelling to an Adam fireplace – as well as a seventeenth-century one. It was built during the reign of King James I and a stone on an inner wall bears the date 20th July 1614.

The house existed when Oliver Cromwell's troops were stationed in town and post-civil war was bought by the Revd Dr Thomas Hurst, rector of Barrowby and Leadenham. When Dr Hurst took residence in 1653, there was a deer park at the rear, which extended to what is now Prospect Place.

Hurst was chaplain to Charles I and as this was essentially a Parliamentarian town, there was little sympathy for him. He was robbed, jailed and ejected for his loyalty to the king.

The last occupant, Miss Kathleen Farish, who had lived there with her sister Gwendoline, left the house for use as almshouses after her death in 1980.

The house had been owned by the Hurst family for several generations, followed by the Fitzalan Howards (Dukes of Norfolk). The Farish family, dealers in Scotch woollen cloth, bought the house in 1883 when the bay windows and stone porch were added. The Misses Farish ran a private school there from 1930s to 1960s.

It is probable that what we call the front today was once the back of the house, the front overlooking the parkland. A stone plaque reads 'T A 1653', for Thomas and Ann (Hurst), although the date is likely to be that of the extension.

The rear of the White House (Misses Farish Almshouses).

An original fireplace inside the White House (Misses Farish Almshouses).

Hurst Almshouses

Dr Hurst also gave houses overlooking St Wulfram's churchyard to home eight poor widows in his will of 1671. They also benefited from the wills of Francis Trigg and Anthony Acomes, and Arabella Langwith. Six senior almspersons were paid a sum not exceeding 6/1d (30p) nor less than 3/6d (17.5d) per week.

The building we see today dates from the nineteenth century, after the original sixteenth-century ones were demolished.

Faraday House

Faraday House, Chambers Street, is the home of the Grantham Freemasons.

The building, which dates from 1883, was originally Faraday House School, a boarding and day school for between fifty and sixty boys.

In the early 1900s it became the Grantham Training Lodge for Young Servants, later known as the Training Lodge for Girls. It has also been an orphanage.

Still known as Faraday House, it was taken over by the Grantham Freemason's Lodges in 1935, after leaving their London Road premises, and was modified for use as the Masonic Hall. They had previously been on St Peter's Hill.

Freemasonry had been practised in Grantham as early as 1726. A petition in 1791 to Grand Lodge requested a lodge to meet in the George Inn.

Above: Inside the Masonic Lodge, Faraday House, Chambers Street.

Left: Symbols on the former Masonic Lodge, behind a building on private land in Bath Street.

Above left: The Grantham American Red Cross Club at the Priory, Union Street, in the Second World War.

Above right: The garden folly called St Egelwyne's Priory. The colour picture shows details of it today, while the bottom image shows it in around 1900.

No Faith in the Priory

The Grade II-listed building, built around 1800, was known as The Cottage until it was bought by draper Arthur Chambers in around 1870, who renamed it St Egelwyne's Priory. This was later shortened to The Priory, although it has never had religious links. It was an odd place to build such a grand home, being between the workhouse and a tallow factory. It became Dr Gibbs surgery then the registry office until it moved to Springfield House in 2007. It is now prestige offices.

In the past, historians have been fooled by the ruins in the garden. They were built not by the Franciscan friars but by local builder Joe White as a garden feature for Mr Chambers.

Pig Was a Swine of a Tavern

Partly in Vine Street, the Blue Pig is one of the town's oldest buildings – but not the oldest pub. In fact there is no evidence that it was a licensed premises until 1826 and is probably a range of cottages that were converted.

Yet it hid its Tudor secret for centuries. It wasn't until 1925, while examining the building for internal improvements, that architect Wilfred Bond discovered it was originally a stone building with an oak-framed upper storey. The stone walls were uncovered and pointed while the timbers in the upper storey were exposed and the spaces plastered. It turned one of the town's dingiest corners into one of its most valuable assets.

The Blue Pig, Swinegate, in 1932, as the rendering was being removed to expose the timbers beneath.

Only four years earlier, in 1921, it had been recommended for closure by Licensing Magistrates who said either the 'Pig' or the 'Artichokes' should be closed on the grounds of redundancy. They said, 'The Blue Pig is the most undesirable type of house. It has badly arranged rooms, is low, dark and badly ventilated and altogether a building in bad condition. It should be either rebuilt or closed.'

Fortunately, it survived all of these threats, and it was the nearby Artichokes that was demolished.

DID YOU KNOW THAT...?

Landlord Served 'Bad Women'
Blue Pig landlord James Broughton was fined £2 with 11/8d (58p) costs in 1883 despite his denials of running a house of ill repute. Broughton pleaded not guilty of knowingly permitting his pub to be the habitual resort or place of meeting of persons of bad character. Sergeant Gray said over a two-hour period he saw several women of bad character go into the Vine Street pub. He said he saw thirteen 'bad women' enter and stay a considerable time.

The Artichokes pub in the 1920s. The site later became a car showroom. The building on the extreme right is Artichokes House before its half-timbered beams were exposed.

Tudor Splendour Unveiled Late

Like the Blue Pig further along Swinegate, the glory of Artichoke House was revealed rather late.

The pub, which was to the left of the house, closed in 1921 and was later demolished. By the 1930s only the wall and medieval archway to the yard beyond remained together with the house, which by then was a shop. It wasn't until the 1970s that the half-timber frame was revealed.

Stonebridge House

Stonebridge House was built east of the river in 1858 for John Hardy, founder of Hardy & Co Bank, of Westgate. It remained in the Hardy family until 1931 when it was bought by Dorothy Schwind, daughter of Col Hutchinson, a director of the Grantham brewers Mowbray. Mrs Schwind lived there until 1940 when it was commandeered for the Camden High School for Girls.

Stonebridge House in 1940.

The 300 students and thirty teachers spent an early part of the war sharing facilities with the girls of KGGS, while living at Stonebridge, St Catherine's House, and billeted with local families.

It was never intended for them to come to Grantham. They initially went to Rutland in September 1939, but Uppingham School was uncooperative and its boys ordered not to speak to the 'Greenflies'.

Six weeks later they were on their way to Grantham following hard negotiating by the ever-resourceful head teacher, Olive Wright. Miss Wright's stay in Grantham was less happy, slipping on ice in 1940 and breaking her hip.

Stonebridge House was mainly classrooms and accommodation for senior teachers. They also took over KGGS in the afternoon. Some of the girls resided at Stonebridge, while others lodged with families in the town. A few girls reported having to sleep on landings, eating burnt porridge, doing homework to a wireless in the background and having hosts that didn't speak to them. But for most, apart from being divided from their families, they made many friends with KGGS girls and German refugees. And most found Grantham's King School boys were far more sociable than those at Uppingham.

But it didn't last. Grantham became a major target for German bombers and it became more dangerous than Camden, so the school moved again, this time to Stamford.

After the war Stonebridge became Spittlegate Boys' School, while Mrs Schwind donated 'The Paddock' for public recreation.

In 1951 the house was bought for the Lincolnshire Constabulary, although not officially opened as the Divisional Police Headquarters until May 1959. They left for Swingbridge Road in 2008 and Stonebridge was taken over by Grantham College, who continue to develop the campus.

5. In the Name of God

The Glory of Grantham

Dominating the town for nearly a thousand years is the magnificent St Wulfram's Church. It is built on the site of a Saxon Christian church, which may have been dedicated to the same saint.

Today's church was begun in the 1100s. It was a huge building for the time with a typical Norman tower at its centre. Six Norman pillars remain, as do traces of Norman window arches.

The massive church for what was a small town was created, thanks to a number of rich wool merchants in the area. Giving money to build another part of the church was, to their way of thinking, one way of ensuring their place in Heaven.

Building the church was a daunting task. Wooden poles lashed together with ropes was the scaffolding; tools were basic hand tools – axes, hammers and chisels. The rest was all down to human skill and energy. Many men spent their lifetime working on the building. When the tower and spire were completed in 1300, it was then the tallest building in the country.

St Wulfram's in 1797 by J. M. W. Turner.

The crypt beneath St Wulfram's Lady Chapel. There is a second staircase to the outside, designed for pilgrims and accessed through a door with three locks and a secret bolt. Before its restoration in 1898, the crypt had been used variously as a vestry, a charnel house and a lumber room.

Trigg's Library, over the South Porch.

Many fittings, carvings and books were burned in a huge fire at the Market Cross in the sixteenth century, after images were banned in churches by Elizabeth I. In 1643 the Roundheads took more wood for fires.

A relic of St Wulfram – an arm – is said to have been stored in the church since a fire at Crowland Abbey, but disappeared during the Reformation.

One of its many attractions is the Trigg chained library created in 1598, which has the distinction of being the first provincial town library under the control of the local authority. Francis Trigg, rector of Welbourn and mayor of the borough of Grantham, donated the original books. He did not want them to become the private library of clerics and scholars, although they were not available to everyone as in the sense of today's public library. The door to the library over the south porch was kept locked and readers needed special permission. Philosopher Henry More, a former King's School pupil, added copies of his works in the late 1600s. Of the books surviving, eighty-three have their original chains. The library includes a legal book printed in Venice in 1472. All 340 books were catalogued by John Glenn in 1986.

DID YOU KNOW THAT...?

Fined for Not Praying
Parishioners failing to turn up for worship at St Wulfram's during any month in 1559 faced a shilling (5p) fine. This increased to £20 in 1581.

ENGLAND'S TALLEST SPIRES

1	Salisbury Cathedral	404 ft
2	Norwich Cathedral	315 ft
3	St Walburge, Preston	309 ft
4	St James Louth	295 ft
5	St Mary, Redcliffe	292 ft
6	St Wulfram, Grantham	282 ft
7	St Elphin, Warrington	281 ft
8	St Botolph, Boston	272 ft
9	St Mary, Kensington	271 ft
10	Chichester Cathedral	269 ft

DID YOU KNOW THAT...?

Chimes of the Times
A clock and quarter jack were installed at St Wulfram's in 1876. The chimes were sounded every fifteen minutes. For eighty years it meant the verger had to climb eighty steps each day to turn the key 210 times until an electric winder was fitted in 1956.

DID YOU KNOW THAT...?

England's Oldest Hippo
The oldest stone carving of a hippopotamus in the UK is believed to be in St Wulfram's Church. It is at the base of an arch in a window in the Lady Chapel and dates from the 1200s.

DID YOU KNOW THAT...?

Tolled Off

St Wulfram's Society of Change Ringers was formed in 1781, making it one of the oldest bell-ringing societies in the country.

The belfry in St Wulfram's Church. (Photo courtesy of Darren Eaton)

They Tried to Nick Our Spire!

Londoners tried to steal St Wulfram's spire to replace the one at St Paul's Cathedral, London. Or that's the rumour that spread through the land.

According to a sixteenth-century book, they wanted it to replace their 160-foot wooden spire, which had burned down in 1561. Written by Barnaby, described as a drunken wit, it tells how a man from London was spotted sketching St Wulfram's spire and when asked, said it was being taken away to be put on the top of St Paul's Cathedral. This created much discussion, including whether there was enough paper to wrap it up.

A contemporary cartoon depicting the theft of St Wulfram's spire.

A wise man settled the dispute by pointing out that there was not enough room to take it down the Great North Road, because of the George inn sign at Stamford, which crossed the road.

St John in Spittlegate

There had long been calls for the parishes of Spittlegate, Houghton and Walton to have their own church. After all, they were separate communities until the Borough Extension Act of 1878 when Grantham swallowed up its near neighbours. The best they got, until early Victorian times, was the southern aisle in St Wulfram's Church.

Building a church in Spittlegate, which was expanding thanks to the new Richard Hornsby Ironworks, looked set to become a reality on Christmas Eve 1839. The vicar of St Wulfram's Canon, William Pochett, told a meeting in the Guildhall that it would cost £3,600 and there was already £2,025 in the building fund. Landowner William Norton offered the land, leaving £700 to find as the Church Building Society would provide the rest.

It was designed by noted architect Anthony Salvin, who had created Harlaxton Manor.

St Anne's

Once Harrowby Road and Dudley Road had been opened by creating St Catherine's Road in 1858, the parish of New Somerby grew at a tremendous pace. Houses were going up everywhere, yet there was no church.

In 1875 the cemetery chapel was acting as parish church, private houses having previously served the purpose. That year Lord Harrowby said he had reserved a piece of land alongside the cemetery for a church to be built in the future. In 1879, a school chapel was built off Cecil Street, on land known as St Anne's Close. It was dedicated to the Mother of the Blessed Virgin.

But the cash-strapped authorities couldn't wait. Instead they built a church of corrugated iron in 1884 across the road, which was formally called St Anne's but generally known as the Tin Tabernacle. It wasn't until 1907 that the brick-built church we know today was opened by the Bishop of Lincoln. It cost £4,000.

Yet until 1962 St Anne's still wasn't quite finished. The back wall facing Hall's Hill was still corrugated iron but at last the church could afford to pay builders the £6,500 required to finish the job.

The original St Anne's Church (right) known as the 'tin tabernacle', which was dismantled and rebuilt in Manchester.

Former Church of the Epiphany, The Grove, Earlesfield, in 2010 shortly before it closed.

Church Left Little Wooden Hut – after Fifty Years

The Church of the Epiphany, on the West Avenue end of The Grove, began in the mid-1920s as a wooden hut bought from Spitalgate Aerodrome in 1926 for £40, which lasted them for nearly half a century. Half an acre of land was bought off The Grove for a further £75. The asbestos internal walls were decorated with cream distemper.

Although improvements were made in the mid-1960s, the church proper was built in 1975, taking only three months. It was forced to close by the district council in 2011 after asbestos was discovered and was subsequently demolished.

Ascension

Lord Brownlow laid the foundation stone for the new Church of the Ascension, Edinburgh Road, in 1954. The new brick-built church, which doubled as a community centre, was paid for by the sale of St Saviour's Church, Manners Street, the foundation stone for which had been laid in 1880 by his grandmother, Countess Brownlow.

The new church, which cost £10,000, replaced the wooden building near Jubilee Avenue, on New Beacon Road. Twelve years after it opened an octagonal-shaped building costing £10,900 was erected as an extension to the dual-purpose church/church hall.

Newly opened Church of the Ascension, Harrowby, in 1956.

St Mary the Immaculate Church

It all began with what is now the Presbytery. It had been built as his home by Grantham grocer Samuel Hand in around 1790, the first building on the west side of North Parade. Some forty years later, theology student Thomas Peter Tempest, of Broughton Hall, near Skipton, was passing along the Great North Road. When he saw Hand's property was for sale, he thought it the ideal site for a Roman Catholic Church, recently permitted under the Roman Catholic Relief Act 1829, and bought it.

The foundation stone was laid in 1831, and the church consecrated in 1833. The original church was a simple, rectangular structure with seating for up to 500 people – ambitious for the likely congregation of the time.

In 1914 painter priest Fr Leo Arendzen took over and served the parish for almost forty years. Leo retired aged eighty in 1953 having raised thousands of pounds for St Mary's by selling his paintings. A painter of great ability, he was the son of an eminent Dutch etcher.

The next major changes to the church came in 1964/65, resulting, essentially, in the structure we have today. The north wall was demolished and another sanctuary was built. The altar was moved to the side of the church so no worshipper was more than 25 feet away. The remaining Bath stone high altar and the Belgian bas-relief stations of the cross became hardcore for the new sanctuary floor.

A series of fourteen paintings of the Way of the Cross, by King's School art master and parishioner Vincent Wells, were added in 1975 and 1990 saw a fifteen-year refurbishment programme, including a comprehensive repair of the outside of the church, new lead work, a new clock after forty years' absence, a recast bell and a new statue of Our Lady above the front door. The interior of the church was redecorated with a remodelling of the sanctuary and the introduction of stained-glass windows.

Inside St Mary the Immaculate Church, North Parade.

DID YOU KNOW THAT...?

Crypt Remains Closed

The original entrance to the crypt in St Mary the Immaculate Church is beneath the western face of the base of the tower. The slab covering it has not been moved often: only in 1835 for the burial of a French emigre priest, Fr Yver; in 1842 for the burials of two children aged six and eight years; and in 1864 for their mother Eliza Theresa Mahon, brought from Greenwich to be buried with them. Why this family were buried there remains a mystery.

Nonconformists

Methodism began in Grantham around 1770 and Charles Wesley paid a visit to town in August 1781. The Wesleyans and Methodists shared a loft over a Welby Street smithy, accessed by a removable ladder. Unfortunately, the farrier had little sympathy for nonconformists and operated his bellows and hammer excessively whenever they met.

The original Wesleyan chapel built in 1803 on the north-west corner of Finkin Street and Elmer Street North.

The first Methodist chapel was built in Finkin Street on the corner of Elmer Street, in 1803, close to the Elmer Street Brewery. It was replaced in a major rebuilding programme across the road in 1827 and is the one we know today as ChristChurch.

The chapel has a lectern dedicated to Margaret Thatcher's father Alf Roberts, who was a lay preacher there.

Congregational Church

The first Independents worshiped in a cottage on the south side of Spittlegate, where Sainsbury's now stands. Their first church was a simple affair, in Union Street, later used variously for Harrison's osiers and latterly an antique centre.

Then, as the Congregational Church, they built a chapel in Chapel Street, which they later sold to the Methodists. In 1870 they completed the Church on Castlegate, which stands today as the Alive Church, on land released by the demolition of Cheyney House.

The first marriage there was in 1871, when Miss Goldie, the pastor William Goldie's sister, was the bride. In the 1970s, nonconformists began to amalgamate and most Congregational Churches merged with others to become the United Reformed Church. In the noughties, there was a local merger with the Finkin Street Methodist Church and they settled together at Christ Church.

The church had been threatened previously, in 1977, when South Kesteven District Council was looking at demolishing the building for improvements to the Castlegate junction. Developers had also been eyeing the rest of the site hoping to build offices.

In 2012 the building was taken over by the Alive Church.

The final day of the URC (formerly Congregational) Church, Castlegate, before amalgamating with ChristChurch, Finkin Street. (Photo courtesy of Mike Matsell)

Harrowby Methodist Church

Harrowby Methodist Church, which began life as a wooden shed (bottom left), became so popular at the turn of the millennium that it was one of the fastest-growing churches in the country.

In 1963 the timber building, which had served them since the estate was built in the 1940s, was replaced by a brick building. The £10,000 improvement was built around the previous one. By the 1990s it was evident that the congregation had even outgrown this one, so an appeal was launched to fund the church we have today. Costing £780,000, it opened in March 2004, a year after the old church closed.

Work continues on Harrowby Methodist Church as a new £10,000 brick building wraps itself around its timber predecessor in 1963.

Inside Bethesda
Evangelical Church, Kitty
Briggs Lane.

Church Built by Devotion

Bethesda Hall is a small independent Christian church on Kitty Briggs Lane run by its brethren. Members take it in turns to preach, without the aid of priests or pastors. It opened in November 1957, having been built as a labour of devotion over four years by multitasking Cyril Jones, who, with volunteer labourers, did the joinery, bricklaying, plumbing and electrics. A special needs teacher at Loughborough College, he lived on Hunt Lea Avenue.

The simplicity of the worshippers is indicated by the church's name. It was never intended to have one, but as Kitty Briggs Lane was yet to be numbered and the post office needed an address, it was called Bethesda – house of kindness.

It was at its peak in the 1970s when more than 100 children from the area would attend the Sunday school and the popular annual outings.

Salvationists Suffered Curfew

The newly formed Salvation Army's first home in Grantham had been the Empire Theatre, George Street, from 1881 to 1884, but their marching through the town riled some people, including the town's leaders. They suffered being stoned in the street and magistrate J. E. Jeans once ordered them to be back in their barracks by 6.30 p.m. They later met at Finkin Street Hall until the Citadel was completed on London Road.

Chief of staff Bramwell Booth visited Grantham to open the new Citadel in 1896. He arrived in Grantham at midnight when many Salvationists assembled to meet him. There was a march through the town and an open-air demonstration in the Market Place.

But it had not started well. When the ground – part of Spittlegate House's extensive gardens – was cleared to make way for the building, a workman clearing trees was seriously injured when a stump fell on him. His left arm was badly injured.

They moved out in 2015, and the building is now used to manufacture Grantham Gingerbreads.

The Salvation Army said farewell to the Citadel, London Road, in May 2015. (Photo courtesy of Dave Jones)

DID YOU KNOW THAT…?

First Marriage Conducted by a Woman

The first marriage in Grantham to be solemnised by a woman was at the Salvation Army Citadel in 1925. It was conducted by Ensign Edith Noakes. She joined together Leicester corps secretary Eva Barker, of Vine Street, Grantham, and William Jones, a bandsman from Cefn, Wales. It was only the third wedding in the thirty-year-old building.

Disillusioned Monks

The Greyfriars, an order of Franciscan monks, had a priory to the west of Market Place, roughly where flats of the same name now exist. From 1290 they had a big influence on the town's development, both spiritually and practically. They brought fresh water to the town via the conduit in Market Place.

The monks also built a church, belfry, cemetery, an aqueduct, gardens, a kiln house, stables and other tenements. But the beginning of the end came in in 1535 with the Reformation. The Greyfriars were investigated by Thomas Manners, Earl of Rutland, who accused the monks of sedition and witchcraft to chief minister Thomas Cromwell.

Over the following three years the priory was closed and like others during the Dissolution of the Monasteries across the country, its assets were seized by the Crown.

6. Transport

Canal Put Grantham on the Map

A Grantham–Nottingham canal taking grain to the city and returning with barges full of coal and fertiliser was first mooted in 1770. The proposal was to make the Witham navigable from Belton Lane bridge to connect it with the Trent. It was abandoned after a survey showed it was unworkable.

Some twenty years later, local businessmen approached canal engineer William Jessop to construct a canal to slash the cost of overland transport. Construction started in 1793, with the first recorded travel in February 1797. The canal reached its peak in 1839, which it maintained until 1851 – the year Ambergate Railway opened.

The Grantham canal was taken over in 1854 by the Ambergate Railway Co. and in 1861 the Nottingham–Grantham railway line was leased to the Great Northern Railway for 999 years and along with it went the canal. Unfortunately, the new owners saw the canal as a cheap competitor to its core business and deliberately ran it down.

By 1917 trade had fallen to a mere 11,000 tonnes and by 1924 the few boats that were still trading found great difficulty navigating due to a lack of maintenance. In 1936 latest owners LNER took out an Act of Abandonment for the total length on grounds that the lock gates were so unsound as to be dangerous and liable to breach.

The Grantham Canal almost dried up in the long summer drought of 1921. By the end of September it was less than a metre wide at the bridge between the gasworks and Shaw's tannery.

The A1 Grantham bypass, opened in 1961, cutting the canal from the town, and the basin at the end of Old Wharf Road was filled in to build industrial units. British Waterways wanted to close it altogether, but was reprieved following protests from anglers and Bjorlow tanneries.

Grantham Canal Restoration Society was formed in the late 1960s, and since then the banks have seen a great upsurge in traffic including walkers, anglers and joggers.

A feasibility study commissioned in 1974 by Grantham Canal Restoration Society estimated that reopening the canal would cost £2,600,000. This would include £200,000 in Lincolnshire, and the opening of a canal basin west of the A1 Grantham bypass.

The canal has been largely cleaned up and lock gates repaired by volunteers, but there is still a long way to go.

DID YOU KNOW THAT...?

Banking on New Canal
Grantham's first bank, the Manners Mansfield Bank, was opened in 1798, to finance the development of the canal and profit from the increase in trade it brought to the town.

DID YOU KNOW THAT...?

Grantham Eel a Record Breaker
A Monster eel caught in the Grantham Canal near Swing Bridge was presented to the Natural History Museum, London, in 1896. Weighing 3.8 kg (8.4 lb) and measuring 1.22 m (48 ins), it was a perfect specimen of a silver eel and the biggest caught at the time.

Ambergate Railway
Little is left of the Ambergate, Nottingham, Boston & Eastern Junction Railway and Canal Co. other than the abutment and part of the embankment near Henry Bell, on Dysart Road. Grantham was something of a slowcoach in terms of railways and the Ambergate Railway from Nottingham to Grantham was the first built after the Stockton and Darlington line to Manchester had been running for twenty-five years. Grantham was a stagecoach town with a lively canal, so there had been little demand.

It had been planned to be 60 miles long, from Nottingham to Spalding with a Sleaford branch of 9 miles from Ropsley and a 20-mile branch from Lenton to Boston. But when it was finished in 1850 the only bit completed was from Colwick to Grantham.

The opening planned for 4 June 1850 was delayed by a month when a government inspector said part of the extensive embankment between Dysart Road bridge and the

Ambergate railway station
off Dysart Road.

Wharf was not consolidated enough. The station, accessed from Dysart Road, had a single platform and the lines ran past it to the gasworks.

From August 1852 the Nottingham trains used the new GNR (current) station, made easy because the route of the GNR line had been deliberately arranged to run as close to the Nottingham line as possible at the Barrowby Road bridge.

By 1890 only the station house and the goods shed remained and these were demolished in the 1960s.

The Great Northern Railway

The Great Northern Railway made a great impact on the town. The Peterborough–London section opened in 1850. Originally, the London–York route was to bypass Grantham to the east, running through Lincoln. Plans then changed to run through east Grantham, following the River Witham, with the station near the Manthorpe Road end of Castlegate.

In the end, the chosen route was more difficult. At Ponton, short cuttings and banks through rocky strata were followed by low-lying land over the Saltersford area where the Witham was crossed by a bridge before the line entered an unstable shale area under Spittlegate Hill.

After passing under the Great North Road at North Parade, the land levelled out until it crossed Grantham Grange district on an embankment where the station was planned, and then on through Great Gonerby to Peascliffe tunnel. The new route was to avoid the historic part of town and to move the line nearer to the Ambergate line with an eye to the future, and build the station in Spittlegate where rates were far lower.

The line opened in 1852, with little celebration. In 1860 a footbridge was erected to avoid danger to the increasing number of passengers having to cross to the down (northbound) platform. In 1862 drinking fountains were installed on the platforms for the use of the poorer classes who could not afford refreshment room prices. In 1878 came the completion of the buildings we know today.

Grantham became the first stop for main line expresses from London, gradually ousting Peterborough as an engine changing post, partly as a result of various branch lines converging near to Grantham.

Above: The former marshalling yards off Springfield Road.

Left: On a cold January day in 1964 British Rail blew up the coaling tower, which had fuelled the steam locomotives since it was built in 1937. (Photo courtesy of Peter Nicholls)

The GNR became LNER (London & North Eastern Railway) in 1923 and BR (British Railways – later British Rail) on nationalisation in 1948. In the mid-1990s privatisation, the infrastructure came under Railtrack (later Network Rail) with individual franchisees running the services.

Cuts by Dr Beeching in the 1960s saw the end of the Grantham–Lincoln line and steam power was replaced by diesel. In 1965 the stretch between Peterborough and Newark was upgraded for high-speed trains (HST). The Grantham stretch was electrified in the late 1980s.

Further improvements came in 2006 when Allington Chord was constructed, allowing service between Nottingham and Skegness to call at Grantham without having to use the East Coast Main Line, allowing an extra twelve trains a day on the main line.

DID YOU KNOW THAT...?

Grantham Loos Made the Charts

Graffiti on a toilet door at Grantham station in 1995 inspired a song by top band Blur. Lead singer Damon Albarn spotted the writing in the gents and used it in Mr Robinson's Quango, on the band's Great Escape album. He was waiting for the London train after visiting his grandparents in Grantham. It read, 'I'm wearing black French knickers under my suit and I've got stockings and suspenders on, I'm feeling rather loose.'

The Queen's Flying Visit

Grantham's great and good were at the station in September 1855 when Queen Victoria made a whistle-stop visit.

The mayor, Robert Azlack White, councillors, magistrates with the officers of the corporation and clergy of the town and members of the nobility were there, but the press and public were left in the cold. Even though the railway company had given 800 platform tickets to the mayor for the occasion, there were many complaints about their distribution.

The royal party, including Prince Albert, the Prince of Wales and the Princess Royal, left King's Cross at 8 a.m. and arrived at Grantham punctually at 10.20 a.m. The mayor addressed Her Majesty, saying, 'Grantham will support the country in the prosecution of the war (Crimea).'

A few minutes after the address, the train moved off to applause.

Grantham Journal editor Joseph Rogers was furious with the mayor as neither he nor any reporters were invited to the event. He said, 'This neglect would scarcely have occurred in any other town in England.'

Grantham bus station, St Peter's Hill, in the 1930s. (Photo courtesy of David Kettle)

Terminus Keeps on Moving

Until the bus station which ran from Welham Street to St Peter's Hill was opened in 1933, the northern end of London Road served the purpose. Of course, it was only a street with no other services. The new place had a kiosk for fruit and other refreshments as well as covered waiting rooms and standing shelters.

It served the town well until the district council took over the land to build more offices and a chamber for itself, so in 1984 a newterminus was incorporated into the Isaac Newton Centre, on Wharf Road.

Grantham Gets a Bypass

It seems hard to believe now, but in 1958 nearly every car, van and lorry travelling between London and the north-east came through Grantham. There was a bit of respite in 1959 when the M1, Britain's first motorway, opened, but the real benefit came three years later.

The £2 million western bypass, which took the A1 from Little Ponton to Gonerby Moor, meant hundreds fewer vehicles going through the town centre every hour, leaving the town comparatively deserted. In June, main contractors Robert McGregor had established a new British record there, laying 425 m of carriageway in a day. Workmen reached their target with twenty minutes to spare.

In an unofficial census, motor dealer Aubrey Musson counted 648 vehicles travelling though Great Gonerby on the Sunday before it opened. The following week it was down to 104 vehicles including eleven lorries. There was not a single accident in the first eight days.

Yet it could have been better had it not been for discerning truckers. Many long-distance lorry drivers shunned the newly opened Grantham road to eat at the popular Tony's Cafe

Grantham A1 bypass at the A607 Harlaxton Road junction being built in 1961.

on Spittlegate Level. So the county council encouraged owner Tony Wakley to move his cafe to Gonerby Moor. A county council traffic survey had revealed 30 per cent of all lorries using the Great North Road (A1) stopped at Tony's.

After first turning down the new site the council said it was a special case and he could move after all. The twenty-four-hour cafe served up to 4,000 meals daily.

The Other Bypass

Once the north-south bypass was up and running and proving a great success, many thought it was only a matter of time before the east-west road (A52) would be built. Instead, much effort and millions of pounds were spent on a fruitless task.

In the 1950s, Princess Drive was designed to take A52 traffic to New Beacon Road and Harrowby Road with a link from roughly what is now Barrowby Gate roundabout, but it fell by the wayside. An alternative £3 million road was due to start in the 1970s but in 1976 the county council put it on hold for seven years. In the County Plan of 1978, it was top priority and expected to be completed in ten years. A cut-price scheme costing £500,000 was mooted in 1985, adapting Harlaxton Road, Springfield Road, Bridge End Road and Somerby Hill. More than 1,000 residents signed a petition saying 'no'.

To celebrate the millennium, highways chiefs agreed the preferred route was to put a junction at Gorse Lane with the A1 near the cricket ground and cross the Witham Valley to join a roundabout close to Prince William of Gloucester Barracks, Somerby Hill.

In the end, a similar route was constructed to the south of Gorse Lane, beginning in 2015 but halting in 2017 for major repairs to the A1. It is due to resume in 2018.

7. Into the Suburbs

Estate Built to House New Workforce

A deal brokered by the town council between Ruston and Hornsby, Barford and Perkins and Aveling Porter in 1933 led to the formation of Aveling Barford, on Houghton Road, which moved its roadroller manufacturing from Rochester, Kent.

To accommodate the new arrivals, a 'garden village' was built off Springfield Road to house 120 families, on allotments east of Rudd's brickyard. It was called Walton Gardens after the former parish on which the houses were built.

The occupiers of the first four houses built in 1934 was decided by ballot. Mr E. Barford, son-in-law of Lord Ashfield, who inspected the new houses, said they were of the best possible design and quality.

Homes Built as Bombs Fell

Health and safety were uppermost in the minds of builders when they erected Beeden Park, off Dysart Road, for these homes were built in the early 1940s when air raids were common in the town. The homes were of the most modern design, with flat roofs. Each house had front and back gardens, with a large central playing area and trees in the street. The first completed were for workers associated with the war effort. They were built by Hustwayte, of Nottingham, for £128,487. Known as both the Flat Tops or Garden City, the estate was officially called Beeden Park after Alderman Harry Beeden.

Beeden Park under construction during the Second World War.

But not everyone was happy with them. In 1944 one resident complained, 'There are 700 new residents up here and no phone box for them to ring the doctor. The town centre has two kiosks at the bus station and one across the road at the post office as well as a phone inside.'

In 1988 they were 'flat-tops' no more, following a £309,000 programme of improvements which included pitched roofs.

Earlesfield Estate Dates from the 1920s

Earlesfield estate began in 1920 with sixteen houses on The Avenue, by Rudd of Wharf Road. There were four pairs and two blocks of fours. Weekly rents varied from 13/6d (67p) to 16/- (80p) including rates.

It made fairly slow progress, delayed by a shortage of bricklayers and the council preferring to develop Harrowby. But as Harrowby filled, attention returned to Earlesfield in the late 1950s with an explosion of public housing for rent in the area.

The first batch of 103 were built by W. J. Roberts, of Bottesford. They were finished in 1961. The rent was £2 13s 0d (£2.65) including rates.

As work progressed, Trent Road finally linked up with Harlaxton Road, near the Isaac Newton pub, in 1981.

A survey in 1996 revealed 85 per cent of residents blamed crime, vandalism, roaming gangs of children and a lack of leisure activities for the estate's problems. A quarter of the town's jobless lived on Earlesfield and 40 per cent of homes had no wage earner. Twelve per cent were one-parent families. Half of the families had no car compared to 25 per cent in Lincolnshire as a whole.

Newly built The Avenue in the 1920s.

DID YOU KNOW THAT...?

First Estate Phone Box
The first telephone kiosk on Earlesfield was erected on the forecourt of No. 19 The Drive, in 1933.

Hill View adventure playground in 1976.

Every Child's Favourite Place

Residents on Earlesfield estate were dismayed when they were told by the district council in 1974 that it was to scrap plans for the proposed Hill View adventure playground.

Playgroup leader A. I. R. Norman said, 'If all the children went to the Meres playing field at the same time, they would be lucky to get on a swing or a slide every other day.' But the council had underestimated the people, and especially the children, who lived there. The kids took over the site of the demolished Hill View workhouse and created their own. Using old pallets, corrugated sheeting, felt and carpets they managed to make a waterproof structure, which they furnished with old chairs and sofas people had thrown out.

The county council was far from happy about this initiative. In 1980 they sent in the bulldozers after a safety inspector said it was too dangerous. In return, they installed a concrete building and a five-a-side soccer pitch. It remained a popular venue for children, who had by now lost the Meres playing field to the formal fee-paying development of an indoor bowling club and a football stadium.

In 1999 it was closed for good following health scares. The county council cleared the land when asbestos was discovered, and said they found the ground also contained arsenic.

Convicted Fraudster Built Estate

An ambitious housing scheme was launched by financier Ernest Terah Hooley, of Long Eaton, in 1934. He bought 16 hectares of land opposite the workhouse on Dysart Road to develop housing, which he planned to rent out at between 55p and 67p per week. The first tenants moved in just before Christmas. The owner also offered a hectare of land for use as a children's playground. He named the roads of the new estate after towns on the Isle of Wight.

Hooley was a man with a magnetic personality and abundant business acumen, but he was also a fraudster. He floated companies that went on to become renowned brands including Raleigh, Schweppes, Dunlop and Bovril, and at the end of the nineteenth century he was a multimillionaire. He bought a 1,183-acre deer park in Manchester and built Trafford Park estate, the world's first industrial park.

Hooley had been declared bankrupt in 1898 with a personal deficiency of £1.5 m. A land transaction led to his ultimate disgrace in 1911. It was a relatively minor offence but he was convicted and sentenced to 12 months' imprisonment. Nine years later, an illegal company flotation landed Hooley back in prison for three years for a further fraud.

There is nothing to suggest his investment in Grantham was anything but straightforward. He died penniless of bronchitis in 1947.

Spittlegate Mill

Spitalgate (or Spittlegate) Mill was called Basker's in the nineteenth century after its owner John Basker, and later Swallow's Mill. Like the other three watermills in town, it was originally a corn mill producing either flour for bakers or malt for brewers.

The original mill dates from the ninth century and is mentioned in the Doomsday Book as 'the cornmill on the southern side of the township of Granta'. By 1750 it was owned by Joseph Manton and it was he who expanded the mill into the Georgian building we know today. His sons John and Joseph became top gunmakers, their customers including King George III.

Much of the mill was gutted in a blaze during the 1890s but repaired and continued as the town's last mill. Joseph Wildes was miller from 1906 to 1915 when Frank Swallow took over. The iron mill wheel fitted in 1886 remains there today.

Rear of Spittlegate (Swallows) Mill, still a working mill in 1955.

After the mill closed in the 1960s, it was converted into a restaurant and nightclub in 1973 which included a glass dance floor over the river and waterwheel. But the final stage, turning it into a hotel, failed when three years later the owners went bust. It was bought by Vacu-Lug for prestige offices and tastefully developed, but the company moved out in 1990.

In 1994 work began converting the mill and mill house to residential use and for new homes to be built on the banks.

Grantham's Oldest Resident

The oak tree (formally Quercus robur) on Belton Lane is probably the oldest living thing in the town. It is believed to be around 750 years old, which means it was planted in the reign of Edward I and his wife Eleanor of Castile. It is possible it was a sapling when he brought her body from Lincoln to London, building Eleanor crosses en route.

The houses forming a crescent around the tree were built in 1948 by apprentices of local builders Fosters. It was next door to a wartime shadow factory run by the Ministry of Aircraft Production and later a branch of Vacu-Lug.

Folly at the Mill

Like other watermills in Grantham, Harrowby Mill became better known by its last owner, George Willoughby.

The mill itself was knocked down in the early twentieth century, but the name now refers to the mock-Tudor mill house. The Grade II-listed house dates from 1702 but wasn't half-timbered and plastered externally until 1898.

And it's not just the Tudor that's mock. The ancient ruins in the garden are just as false, built by Joe White for Mr Willoughby – who owned the Little Dustpan in Westgate. Mr White also built the Priory 'ruins' in Union Street.

A sketch of the old Harrowby Mill by R. L. Harris. It was knocked down in the early twentieth century.

Princess Drive waiting to be surfaced in 1953. The road was designed to be part of a ring road for Grantham.

Work Begins at Harrowby

A start was made on building hundreds of new council homes in 1952 as the town grew closer to Belton Park. It began with Princess Drive and the following year, parallel road Queensway was also named after Her Majesty following the coronation.

Other roads were Ash Grove and Almond Grove. Six roads built in 1954 were named after Australian and New Zealand towns visited during the year by the Queen.

Also that year, Selleck Nicholls, of St Austell, Cornwall, built fifty-two Cornish unit houses near Edinburgh Road and north of Queensway for £73,699.89. It was called Cornwall Close.

Building on the Tennyson Avenue area, known as Cherry Orchard (or Holt), had begun in the 1930s.

Arnoldfield House

Arnoldfield, or Arnold House as it was originally called, was built in 1820 by William Ostler JP, a solicitor who took an active part in Grantham's local affairs. He was variously the Town Clerk and Mayor of Grantham.

The next owner was Joseph Wilders and in 1872 it became known as Arnoldfield House. In 1920 it was bought for £6,500 by former amateur jockey and horse breeder Vincent Hemery, who also owned two fruit farms in Jersey.

After the Second World War Arnoldfield was unoccupied until acquired by Aveling-Barford, who converted it into flats for visiting businessmen. It was also occupied by several company personnel as a temporary home until in 1963 it became the work's social club. A spacious assembly hall was added for dances, stage shows and parties.

The estate became sports fields and home to Aveling Barford gala. It also hosted one of the biggest sports festivals seen in the East Midlands in 1985.

But the 1980s were volatile times for Aveling Barford. In 1987, then owner Dr Lee Kin Tat made a huge profit from its controversial sale. His Jersey-based firm Perion bought the 14-acre site from Aveling Barford for £350,000, then resold it to Beazer Homes and Barrett for housing development for £1.5 million.

The house and outbuildings were converted into flats for sheltered housing while an agreement was reached to allow archery, bowls and tennis clubs to remain.

Gonerby House

Grade II-listed Gonerby House, now divided into flats and surrounded by new-builds, has a Jacobean frontage with Victorian wings.

It was the home of former mayor Susan Brace, then became the dormitory for boarders of the King's School until 2002, followed by a spell as house of residence for Grantham College's overseas students. The interior was completely changed but contains the remains of original doorways and cellars. It contains a fire basket with a decorated iron back dated 1724.

Gonerby House in 2002, before it was incorporated into a housing development.

The weir is all that is left of the old paper mill.

Little Left of the Paper Mill – Other than a Fine Walk

Houghton Road once led to the tiny parish of Houghton, which was absorbed into Grantham in 1878. Before the houses were built on land bought from the Earl of Dysart it was called Paper Mill Lane. All that is left of Houghton paper mill is the weir and the diverted River Witham.

At this point the riverbanks have been built up to create a fall for the mill, while the original watercourse acts as an overflow.

The original mill, built in around 1700, was timber, but a major refurbishment in the 1780s saw the three-vat mill housed in brick. The mill frequently changed hands, few making a profit and many ending deeply in debt. It made paper by pulping rags, the river not only supplying the power but also the clean water to wash them.

Industrialist Richard Hornsby and his descendants took it over from 1838 until 1872, making a number of innovative improvements. Under them it produced wrapping paper for grocers.

The last owner was Michael Jack, who concentrated on bowl paper, hosiery cartridges and grocery papers. He closed it in 1890 when one man and two women were still employed. It was knocked down shortly afterwards.

RAF Spitalgate and Prince William of Gloucester Barracks

In August 1914, a biplane and monoplane landed in a barley field off Whalebone Lane, not far from what was to become RAF Spitalgate. The planes were flying from Hendon to Bardney, near Lincoln, but one had been forced to land just across the road from Whalebone Lane.

Months later, work began on a 193-acre airfield, with six hangars and other buildings covering 30 acres. It was a perfect place: the highest ground for miles and very flat, ideal for training young pilots. It opened as Spittlegate (*sic*) aerodrome in 1916 and two years later 856 members of the Royal Flying Corps were stationed there, men who later that year became members of the RAF.

Ten years on, a further 140 acres of land was bought, more buildings were erected and the base was given the new name RAF Grantham. It was the first training station to receive the legendary Tiger Moth.

In 1937, RAF Grantham became part of 5 Group Bomber Command, which set up its HQ at St Vincent's. Unsuitable as a bomber base, it continued just for training.

In the Second World War, Britons were joined by Canadians, Australians and New Zealanders and in 1944 the base was renamed RAF Spitalgate (*sic*).

The officers' mess, Prince William of Gloucester Barracks, in 2010.

One of the original features of RAF Spitlegate at PWGB in 2010.

A big change came in 1960 when the RAF men moved out and a fleet of coaches delivered 350 girls and NCOs of the Women's Royal Air Force (WRAF) from RAF Wilmslow, near Manchester. RAF Spitalgate became the only WRAF depot in the United Kingdom. Girls aged seventeen and over completed six weeks' basic training before moving to specialist training schools. The barrack blocks were redecorated in modern pastel shades with flowered curtains hanging from pelmet rails. The influx was well received by the town's publicans and even more so by its young men.

The station was also HQ of No. 3 Police District, Secretarial Officers School and the RAF Central Gliding School. The WRAF was transferred to Hereford in 1974 while other sections had a year to find a new home.

In 1975, the RAF handed the base over to the Army, who renamed it Prince William of Gloucester Barracks. The old technical and domestic site buildings from the RAF days are virtually all intact and still in use, although the control tower was demolished.

The first 120 Territorial Army volunteers from the Royal Corps of Transport arrived in October 1976. When fully operational there were sixty full-time soldiers and 200 territorials. It became headquarters for the Royal Logistics Corps Territorial Army in April 1993. In 2017 the government announced it was to be closed within a couple of years.

Army Camp Stepping Stone for Tenants

Alma Park gets its name from Alma Wood, planted in memory of Lt Horace William Cust of the Coldstream Guards, who died in 1854 at the Battle of Alma, in the Crimean War.

It was originally built as an extension to Belton Camp during the First World War and included ranges for the Machine Gun Corps to practise. It was also used by the military in the Second World War as there were already some 200 permanent buildings there. Then in February 1942 the RAF Regiment was formed with a training school at Alma Park. Put in charge was Major General Claude Liardet, the Army's Inspector of Aerodrome Defence.

A car rally at Alma Park in 1960, before the homes were demolished.

The former firing range is still a feature in Alma Park Wood.

When the regiment moved to a new home at Catterick in 1946, for a short spell Alma Park was used as a transit camp for German and Italian prisoners of war.

In 1946, Margaret Thatcher's father, Alf Roberts, as chairman of Grantham Borough Council's finance committee, recognised the need for new housing and took out loans totalling £1 million for the area's housing. The council converted the Alma Park buildings for civilian use at a cost of £350 each, turning 59-ft-long buildings into two-bed semi-detached bungalows. The 35-ft buildings were converted to three-bed detached bungalows. In all, 114 family units were created for the 1,700 people on the housing list.

Five years later, the residents were far from pleased. They said they were living in disgraceful and deplorable conditions. Apart from inferior interiors, they said there was a lack of amenities at the estate, known locally as 'Heartbreak Corner'. One tenant said how he had pulled two children from a static water tank on the site. There was also concern that a twenty-month-old child had been killed by a van, as the homes had no fences. Tenants also condemned damp rooms, poor maintenance, no facilities, no bus service and the lack of street lighting.

It was approached from Harrowby Lane by a 'cinder path' and a few planks acting as a bridge over the Witham brook. The nearest pub was the Three Gables, Signal Road, with the Waggon and Horses, Manthorpe Road, second closest. The houses were government owned until 1953, when they were sold to Grantham Borough Council for £17,500.

In 1960, it was decided not to replace existing tenants as they moved out, and commercial tenants moved in with Mitchell & Barrett Packaging Limited (later Barpak) among the first.

Acknowledgements

The author would like to thank all the people and organisations that made this book possible, either indirectly or supplying information and illustrations: Anglian Water, Malcolm Baxter, Buckminster Estates, Peter Burrows, Camden School for Girls, Fr Stuart Cradduck, Ruth Crook, Darren Eaton, Vaughan Hardy, Jill Harrison, James Herdman, Robert J. Hirst, *Grantham Journal*, Grantham Library, Grantham Museum, Jane Green, Graham Jeal, Dave Jones, Malcolm G. Knapp, David Kettle, Fred Leadbetter, Walter Lee, Mike Matsell, Amy McNamara, Peter Nicholls, Sue Redmile, Angela Shields, Eric Summers, Sleaford Library, and Chris Windows.

About the Author

John Pinchbeck is not only Grantham-born, but can trace his male line back to the mid-seventeenth century in the town. He became interested in local history when leafing through old editions of the *Grantham Journal* while working there. Even when he moved on to the *Lincolnshire Echo* and *Sleaford Standard*, he continued browsing the old *Stamford Mercurys*, which covered Grantham in pre-journal times.

Firstly, he self-published the *Grantham in the News* series, followed by commissions for *Changing Face of Grantham*, *Grantham in Focus* and *Grantham Through Time*.

On retirement, he started a website for people to post old photographs. This proved so popular that it developed into 'GranthamMatters' – now carrying news and comments as well as the popular 'Grantham Past' section – and now attracts more than 10,000 visitors every day.

Secret Grantham is his thirteenth publication (including two heavily revised editions of previous books).